THE GREATNESS FACTOR

an auminimua expression

UNIVERSAL PUBLISHING CO.

Eugene, Oregon

ISBN 0-9622035-0-5

First printing April 1989
1 2 3 4 5 6 7 8 9 0

Manufactured in the United States of America

UNIVERSAL PUBLISHING CO.
P.O. Box 10121
2351 Ironwood Street
Eugene, OR 97401

Table of Contents

DEDICATION

To Rani and other parts of my Self who recognized the validity of what was being said and gave their encouragement and support to this expression. Without their faith this book may never have been written.

ON AUTHORSHIP

Because of the nature of this material, I have experienced a reluctance to declare authorship. The dividing line is thin between what may be seen as the work of an individual and the work of that which is the collectivization of individuals. An individual does not really work alone. For instance, it is not the individual who created the alphabetic symbolism with which he works nor has he coined each word and formed each phrase. Rather, one works with a system through which one is continuous with other individuals operating within a framework of understanding that is bounded and declared by a Greater Self.

On the one hand, there is nothing separate or individual. On the other, individuals apply themselves to their callings using tools generated by countless other individuals and extend that which they are called to extend.

It has been my intention to offer this explanation of existence in such a way that it could be acceptable to the greatest number of people. There are myriad reasons for rejection but only one for acceptance exists. That is because the thoughts and ideas strike home, because there is a truth common to basic understanding and because the reader's main interest is in finding and following Truth wherever it may appear.

A writer deserves neither praise nor condemnation any more than a pen, typewriter or other device through which ideas are conveyed to the public. I offer a name that was given socially for those who consider this important or feel the urge to investigate further.

When we play the game of authorship, asking, "Who is the

author? You or someone else?" pretending that there is separation between individuals and between works, then, I must admit, "I am the author."

Of course, both you and I know that The Real Source is a place in Mind where we can all listen and hear The Music of The Universe.

For those who find the information herein beneficial, I apologize for having taken so long to deliver it. Some of us stumble about a lifetime before finding the path (only to realize that we were on the path all along).

I offer these thoughts for your appraisal, acceptance, rejection, refusal, praise, ridicule or whatever. You are The Creator in Action. As you declare it to be, so it is.

Paul J. Lehman, scribe

PREFACE

THE GREATNESS FACTOR is an invitation to reach for your own knowledge. What you, yourself, know goes far beyond anything that you have been taught or what anyone else can tell you.

Somewhere in the depths of your being lies the answer to all questions about existence. When one truly chooses to know rather than idly speculate or be guided by the intrigues of mystery, these answers become obvious.

In this book I have tried to express how we create our personal reality, what keeps us from being in touch with the underlying Truth of Our Existence, and how to transcend conditions of petty conflict that keep us from recognizing our greatness.

The purpose of this book is not to tell you something that you do not know but rather to remind you of what you already know and help you arrange that knowledge so that you can be more creatively effective and experience a greater enjoyment of life.

This information has been transcribed to transport you systematically from the lesser self, the mental arrangement with the greatest amount of conflict and the least amount of power, to the Greatest Self, the mental arrangement with the least amount of conflict and greatest amount of power. We all operate somewhere along this path of growth and knowledge. It is important that you do not discourage and confuse yourself by looking too far ahead or bore yourself by not getting beyond the initial revelations. Allow your interest to be your guide. It is far wiser than you suspect.

In writing this, I have tried to anticipate reasons for automatic rejection. Unfortunately, even that could, for someone, be a reason. There are those of us who are always reviewing works of this nature, looking for a reason to condemn them or avoid them. I know, because at times I have been that type of reviewer and done so.

Perhaps, I was not yet ready to recognize and accept deeper truths. We are only able to grow spiritually as our understanding permits. If you feel too uncomfortable at any time when you are reading this material, rest for a while, do something else. Your understanding can wait.

There are no short cuts to greater knowledge. Your heightened awareness depends on your willingness and ability to process the information that will enable you to modify your mental arrangement. This means that, as you begin to recognize the truth of your existence, your personal reality will change. You will no longer need to hold fast to ideas that cause you trouble and conflict robbing you of your natural power.

This, or any other book, can only be a tool to aid you in that process. Do not make any expression so important that you recite it rather than realize its message. By doing so, you fail to receive its benefit.

Finally, be cautious and conscientious in your development. It is said that a little knowledge is dangerous. The conflicts and conflagrations of the world are always caused by those operating from little knowledge believing that they have great knowledge. They usually destroy themselves and many others through ignorance of their own operation. Do not allow yourself to become demented by early revelations. There is far to go and much to know before you can act from knowledge and wisdom.

Chapter I

THE CAUSE OF KNOWING

The human mind continually reaches out for new experiences and new insights. That is its nature. It is always groping for that which will complete its potentiality. It has no other purpose and no other reason for existence. You may say immediately, "I am not going to read any farther, this premise is completely destructive of what I now know and believe." In the world you have constructed, this would seem true. In stabilizing the direction you have chosen to grow and explore, you may have set up a system for automatic rejection of every expression not similar or along that path. Yet, it is because of your groping and reaching in a chosen direction that you find reasons for rejection of other expressions.

You may say, "That's interesting but I'll wait and see if it is really an accurate statement." You may be a bit cautious about what you include in your *mental arrangement*. There are and have always been people with little or no insight who would mislead you. How can you be sure that this is not another? Even if everything offered is accurate, how can you be sure that it has value? Most assessments of value are based on whether or not an expression will aid you in the direction you have already chosen to go. These are subordinate choices. The fact is, you have chosen to grow and extend in some direction. Your interest is the real measure of value.

You may say, "That is absolutely true, but the problem is that there are so many expressions and so many things that I am interested in. I mean, there is no way that I can possibly follow them all." Many of us create a world of bits and pieces never realizing that they are a part of some greater whole.

1

Instead of recognizing the place where all the "pieces" fit together we are confused and disturbed by thefragments. Here, there is a tendency to become involved in one expression after another, never recognizing the similarities that lead toward **The Underlying Truth** but only the shallow differences that lead toward conflict and confusion. The problem is that you have no means of deciding which expressions are beneficial, which are merely a waste of time and which are really harmful or misleading.

In any case, there is, in your mind, a *yardstick* with which you measure all expressions, judging them for accuracy and evaluating them for practicality. It is you who decides the direction and who makes the judgments. It is you who gauges the extension and the path along which this extension will take place.

This *yardstick,* your means of measure, may have been handed down for generations and bequeathed to you by your parents. It may be something your parents or forebears developed to defend themselves against harsh discipline and unyielding domination. It may be something you developed through your interaction with the circumstances of the world.

Whatever the cause and whatever the condition, *your yardstick is only as accurate as you, yourself, have allowed it to become.* If you have never looked at the device with which you measure the world and with which you judge others, you have only the accuracy that was developed in it by your ancestors or some other authority from which you received it. *All that you see in life as difficult, frustrating, frightening or confusing is the result of working with a faulty yardstick.*

Awareness, wisdom and knowledge result from improvement of the *yardstick* with with one measures the world, oneself and others. No matter how accurate you consider your *yardstick* to be, it can always stand improvement. If you do intend to improve it, you must always be willing to gauge its accuracy against other *yardsticks* that seem to work well. Whenever you find that you must defend your measuring device because you fear that it will be undermined, be made inconsequential, or shown to be inaccurate by the measuring device of another, it is wise to set your measuring device aside for a time and learn of the accuracy of the overpowering measuring device. It is through doing this that growth happens and peace is assured. Sometimes we find our method of measurement better and more accurate. Sometimes we find the *yardstick* of another superior and adopt it as our own. More probably, we find that the *yardstick* that is most successful is the combination of the two in question.

Here is the beginning of the path toward wisdom. It is the ability to transcend the invitation to fight over petty differences and recognize some underlying truth that is inclusive of disparate viewpoints. This is the cause of real knowledge. Herein is an inoculation of pure understanding that immunizes the participants against the mental disease of lesser viewpoints and less accurate measuring devices.

The cause of knowing begins basically with the decision that one does not know absolutely, without error, anything. It is the realization that anything known can be better known and that anything decided can be redecided. It is not until one realizes this that one is capable of new growth and new insight.

Without the world of material and circumstance, knowing has no purpose. It has value only when there is an interaction between material and material, circumstance and circumstance or material and circumstance. It is here that decisions are made and action begins.

What is generally termed "knowing" or "knowledge" is merely a recall from memory of the impression induced by material or circumstance. Here, "knowledge" is shallow and informational, based on social decision and has no universal validity. The "knowledge" drawn on in "small talk" and other social conversation is usually of this nature. What is witnessed is the effect of social decision, not the cause. In other words, the cause of social conversation is social decision.

One might ask then, "What is the cause of social decision?" The answer is, "The greater decision to stabilize **Real Knowledge** and create a society." Those laying social "cornerstones" see themselves as creating order from chaos. It is their decision that directs the society. Those joining or "drummed into" the society operate from the established decisions and have no real voice in the society's operation. Here is the dividing line between rulers and subjects.

Those operating from the *mental arrangement* of subject have no ability to see beyond the borders of the incorporating decisions. Their reality is fixed by social process and their understanding limited to what the elders of the society feel is comfortable for social well-being. The "truth" for those with a subjective *mental arrangement* is what the social leaders proclaim to be "true."

It is usual, in establishing social truth, to proclaim some terrible thing that will happen if followers do not conform. It is also common practice to state that there is a reward for conforming. A third cornerstone is the establishment of an ideal. This gives the participants something to strive for and hopefully achieve. The object is to keep the subjects' attention focused in a direction which the founders see as progressive.

Most social members choose willingly to abide by the principles and rules that have been established. Without this happening, the fabric would decay and the participants would go their separate ways. Their choice to participate in the decisions that are instituted makes the society viable. Those who come later and do not participate from choice must be persuaded and kept in line by whatever means the society has adopted to maintain its structure.

One of the principal "truths" that is used for social construction is the idea of "death." The fear of dying is the single most useful tool in establishing social order. By encouraging this natural fear, those who govern are able to keep their subjects aligned with the principles that they have set forth. Fear of capture and imprisonment works here as well.

For those who see through these arbitrary limitations and say, "So what, we are all going to die anyway," or "They can imprison my body but they cannot imprison my mind," a secondary fortification against the decay of social process is established. This draws on another of our natural human fears, "Fear of the Unknown".

That which is "known", sensed, witnessed or established is one thing but that which is "unknown" is quite another. Many societies go to great lengths to promote this fear. "You know and have witnessed death and do not find it fearful?" "Aha, but what happens to you after death?" The sole purpose of this reasoning and logic is to establish limits of behavior and to keep individuals dependable as social members.

The "hereafter" is always imbued with the idea of reward for proper behavior and punishment for improper behavior. Social members use the established ideas to keep one another in line. The more the ideas are used, the more credence they acquire. (For instance, the Christian behavior control method is to state that one will "go to hell" if one does not change one's ways, while Hindus may insist that one will be reborn as a pig.)

In "polite society", those who have accepted and abide by the principles and rules set forth, the motivation is different. Here the main concern is the continuation of established social process with minimum disruption. "Truth" here is the methods and ideas that keep the social fabric from decay into "Chaos". Members at this social level participate in rites and ceremony, not so much because they, themselves, believe in the fabrications that compose the social myths, but rather because they need to set an example. They need others to believe that they believe in them. More often than not, their private lives demonstrate what they really believe.

All societies can be divided functionally and psychologically into three classes. (They could be divided into more or less, but that does not serve the purpose here.) The Upper Class, or establishment, whose function it is to keep the framework workable and intact. The Middle Class, or management, who apply the established principles in business and cultural enterprise. And the Lower Class, or labor, who function in business and cultural enterprise.

For each of these classes, "knowledge" takes a different form. The Upper Class (as stated previously) confines its "knowing" to what will keep the social structure intact. This includes social expansion, defense against the intrusion of other social systems and the reconciling of differences between disputant factions within the society.

The Middle Class confines its "knowing" to how to be more effectively productive, how to compete with other societies in the market place and how to keep laborers comfortable, secure, satisfied and efficient or, in some cases, fearful, cowed and productive, and how to become Upper Class.

The Lower Class confines its "knowing" to how to get the most reward for the least amount of work, how to become middle class, and how to get the maximum pleasure out of life.

For all three classes the cause of "knowing" is different. Within the social framework all knowing is dictated by social needs. Each individual restricts knowing to that which will fill their personal needs, or bring them power and prestige. When social "knowledge" permeates our thought system, controlling our language and directing all our decisions, we are unable to intercept **Real Knowledge.**

It is obvious from this that **The Cause of Real Knowledge** does not lie within the social framework. It is actually oblivious to the social framework and derived from a reality that transcends social concerns. Here, Truth is encountered without concern for consequences. Here, the individual acts from a motivation that causes social participants to retreat in awe.

Is it any wonder that the leaders of a society must rid themselves of this intrusion? Is it any wonder that the management of a society must discredit this outsider or follow to approach **Knowledge** themselves? Is it any wonder that those who labor in the society must support this intruder or run in terror?

A *Person of Knowledge* sees through and beyond the social framework. When such a person appears, changes happen; old systems of order disappear; new systems of order are established.

When a person's *knowledge* is specialized, that is, the person sees through the social framework but in a limited way, society sees that person as special. If it finds use for the unusual talents offered, it declares the offering valuable and the one who makes the offering a genius. If it does not and feels that these talents may disrupt the social process, it declares what is offered, useless or detrimental, and the one who makes the offering, insane.

Everyone has certain talents through which they can express Knowledge in the world of material and circumstance. Society tends to suppress talents that it does not yet understand. It is because of this that the individual who would act from Knowledge and thereby achieve Greatness must recognize the social borders that stultify and impede action in the world of material and circumstance.

The Cause of Knowledge is far beyond anything that can be seen by human eyes, or heard by human ears. It is **The Reality** that is not hampered by human frailties or bounded by social concerns. It is a direct and unrestricted contact with **That Which Knows No Boundaries Or Restrictions.** It is only known by those who are aware of the limitations of the world they hold in memory and are willing to transcend them by changing their *mental arrangement.*

Greatness is the result of operating from this **Inner Knowledge,** trusting it completely and accepting that the circumstance in which you find yourself at this moment is for your benefit and the improvement of your *mental arrangement.*

Your world is as you, and you alone, have arranged it. Like a fingerprint, no two arrangements are exactly alike. Unlike a finger print, you have the possibility of arranging your world differently if it is not bringing you joy and prosperity. *You are directly involved in the Cause of Knowing.* Decisions you make now determine your tomorrow and the tomorrow of the world you witness.

Realizations:

You and I are directly involved in The Cause of Knowing. It is through our decision that the world we witness is the way it is. That to which we attach our attention becomes real for us.

Since realization is the process of making something real and thus creating our personal reality, it behooves us to be in touch with that part of ourselves that is the cause of everything we claim to know. Anything less robs us of our initiative and deprives us of our potential.

Chapter II

THE NATURE OF KNOWING

All knowing can be divided into three modes. First, there is the knowing that supports and maintains the world of material and circumstance. Without this the perceived world would not exist. For a human being this can be witnessed as that inner knowledge which causes, develops, observes and regulates the body. This includes genetic characteristics such as height, weight, musculature and skeletal structure. (Some of these factors can be changed at other levels of consciousness, but only within preset parameters.) This also includes heartbeat, breathing, metabolism and reproductive abilities. (These factors are more consciously accessible as one becomes more creatively aware.) Most of what society describes as instinctive can be attributed to this mode of knowing.

The *second mode of knowing* is that which is socially decided and regulated. (See Cause of Knowing.) Everything involved with acceptable language and behavior is of this nature. Here knowing is confined by projected limits of recognition and acceptability. The more one adheres to social desires, the more one stays within the limits of this knowing. Relying on social "truth" as the guideline for thought and action, the individual arranges talents to fit the social need.

The third *mode of knowing* relies solely on **The Greater Truth.** Seeing through and beyond social decision, a *Person of Knowledge* allows the given talents to flourish and multiply with minimum or no restraint. In doing so the individual grows in knowledge and awareness. This is the only reward a *Person of Knowledge* seeks or needs. Here one does for the sake of doing and is for the sake of being.

No other reason stands in the way of knowing and performance.

Early in life, before the inhibiting influences of family and society begin to mold and form social character, the child operates in the first and third modes of knowing. Here there is a continual reaching out for new possibilities of action as the body grows and responds to the world of material and circumstance. Reality is as the individualizing mind creates it, incorporating sense perceptions and and circumstantial occurrences to form a valid description of the material world. It is from this description that the child begins to operate, unmindful of any other possible reality.

When the child runs into difficulty and the mental image that was constructed proves to be invalid, the child's mind immediately builds another world, projecting new constructs which the mind estimates as able to pass the limitation that it has encountered. New constructs that prove successful are retained; those that fail are abandoned.

This is the continual process in the early life of a child. Truth and Knowledge come to bear here as the child develops a relevant reality. Each new world that is created rises from the ashes of the old world retaining those features that are deemed important, dropping features that are not functional and adding new features that seem to provide greater understanding. From this process the child's reality grows and matures.

Depending on the environment, intention of older family members, (being influenced as much by other family members as they are by their parents) the inner need for creative expression and the acceptability of such expression, a child's reality becomes accurate and successful or distorted and creatively dysfunctional. Here social influences have begun to play a role in the growth of the child's reality.

It is at this point that training begins. This is the changing of the naturally creative investigative self that knows no boundaries or restrictions into a self that is socially functional, socially reliable, socially dependent and socially controllable. It is here that flourishing talents can become stifled and distorted, or abandoned to meet the projected social need. It is here that family and social acceptance become a factor in the personal reality that the child is constructing. Unless there is someone who recognizes, appreciates and encourages them, or unless the inner direction is stronger than the external influences, these talents lose their truth quality, their universal purpose and their function as a supply line for greater understanding in the world.

Unfortunately, each social subgroup tries to capture and proclaim as its own that which it sees as powerful and unique. In attempting to do so it usually destroys the essence of what it has encountered. It is left with a shell from which the kernel has been removed, a butterfly pinned to a board, or the shadow of where something once magnificent stood.

True Knowing cannot be refined or inculcated by a society, it can only be experienced and encouraged. It will find its own way. It will extend as it needs to extend. What others think of it is unimportant. When "what others think of it" becomes important, **True Knowing** ceases to exist.

One may think of a child's extending reality as a *Power Spiral.* Reality tends to grow and expand outward and upward as new ideas are projected and new experiences are encountered. Everything that is touched by the ever expanding periphery is an alternative possibility that may be included in the growing reality. While the mind is open it is continually inclusive of new ideas and expressions and expands logarithmically. That which has now become familiar is now taken for granted and neglected as consciousness reaches forward for new experiences and expressions.

Social pressures and mores tend to dampen this expansion and, with "proper training" reality is reduced to linear expansion. Those who retain logarithmic expansion are seen as genius, insane or troubled. Those who accept training are seen as dependable, reliable and socially fit. Those who have accepted training and set aside or distorted their talents for social acceptability stand in awe and are cautious of those who have not. It is the wildness and unpredictability of the untrained that they most fear.

Yet, it is not training itself that is detrimental to the knowing. It is the method of training and the motivation of the trainer(s). When the purpose of training is solely to make the individual socially acceptable and responsive, the training usually dampens and destroys the natural enthusiasm that accompanies the release of creative pressure through acting from natural talents. Under these conditions, the real knowing of the person is vilified and subjugated while the social knowing is rewarded and encouraged. For the trainer, the social reality is all that matters. Is it any wonder that many individuals trained thus find their lives unrewarding and unfulfilled?

True training requires the insight and attention of the trainer. Here the trainer recognizes and appreciates the knowing and reality of the person being trained. As the reality grows, the trainer gently guides it into directions that keep it from colliding and conflicting with the reality of others. In this manner the talents are expressed, greater knowing happens, and the individual experiences peace and fulfillment. The society, though it may be disapproving and misunderstanding during the duration of training and operation of the trainee, is richer for the offering.

Talents and knowledge bring to the social world (the world of organized material and circumstance) a quality without which it would wither and die. But then, that which loses contact with **True Knowing** and knows only of proper social action or the consequences of improper social action is already dead or, at least in a sound sleep.

Another factor in *the nature of knowing* is the protective devices that guard knowing against destruction or distortion by "outside" forces. Part of our knowing is assigned to this task. For this discussion we may assign the name *Defense Control Mechanism* or *DCM* for short. As we build our world in early childhood this factor is in our reality as, "What do I control and what controls me?" As we grow these blanks become filled in our *mental arrangement*. We find ways to bypass that which we feel controls us or we allow it to dominate us. We find more ways to be in control or we give more and more control to "others". We find that many things and conditions are neutral, neither controlling nor controllable.

When we are embattled we call on this power automatically. Here knowing is logarithmic and wild. It does not respect ordinary limits and leaps immediately to new possibilities and conclusions reacting to the circumstances that are causing difficulty. Like all reality, this reality expands and extends as we give it power. We are seldom conscious of when our *DCM* moves from defense to attack. In the mind of the beleaguered person there may be only the idea of defense as the "other" is attacked and destroyed.

An aware trainer keeps the trainee's mind conscious of these factors so that conflict is reduced and the energy introduced by adversity is used in a fulfilling, creative way.

15

An unaware trainer punishes the trainee creating a barrier to this creative pressure, frustrating the ability to know and cutting the trainee off from deeper urgings.

The DCM problem is resolved only when the individual learns that perfection of control is acting in such a way that the "adversary" does not experience being controlled but rather being in control.

For most social members, reality expands linearly unless they are thrown into a situation where they must call on this greater ability to survive. For them, comfort, security and, possibly, long life are the most important factors of their existence, followed closely by social image, concern for the security or well-being of others (lest they become a burden) and concern for "the hereafter". Vision here is narrow and suspicious, with members constantly apprising one another of problems and difficulties.

At this basic social level (level 1 in a *hierarchy of awareness**), knowing is confined to small talk. There is no effort to understand, study or change any of the social principles that cause and constitute the basic language. For these individuals, life's *Spiral* has become a *circle of comfort and certainty,* and they do not want it to change. They know "all they need to know" and are extremely cautious of that which is unfamiliar. The tendency here is to associate only with one's own kind and avoid anything that might disrupt the "status quo". They know how the world should be and are continually frustrated and angry when events do not bear out their beliefs.

If a person at level one experiences the urge to know after having been thoroughly indoctrinated by social process and language, there is a complete confusion about how to initiate the knowing process. This person must be able to risk the displeasure of the fellow social members. Investigation of any other belief system is an indication of doubt

*see Appendix I

of the current belief system. Usually the seeker at this level (level two in the hierarchy of awareness*) plays it safe, keeping whatever is investigated at a sufficient distance that it does not really affect the current belief system.

A person at level two awareness looks only for expressions that are mysterious or unexplainable. In this manner the would be seeker avoids anything that might really cause a change of *mental arrangement* or belief system.

To rise to level three in the *hierarchy of awareness** a person must investigate and become a participant in a belief system other than the one in which the initial training took place. It is only then that the seeker can begin to measure early training in social process.

At level four, one is prone to throw away the one training in favor of the other. The reality of a level four person is only able to handle one belief system at a time but is able to switch between them.

There may be more than five belief systems which this individual has encountered and participated in before the searcher begins to combine the tenets and principles of these systems.

When this combination takes place, the searcher rises to level five in the *hierarchy of awareness**. Still acting within the confines of the encountered expressions, the searcher suddenly realizes the underlying cause of all social systems.

When the underlying cause of social systems becomes evident, the seeker reaches a new plateau, level six. All the bits and pieces are suddenly falling into place. Knowing now is approaching logarithmic progression. From here on there is no rest. The law is, "Express or die." But now, death is assured no matter what you do. So you ex-

*see Appendix I

press, simply because you enjoy expressing. What you express is that there is no reason for conflict, that all Truth leads to the Same Reality. You no longer need to have others see as you do because they **are** you being there. The realization leaves you ecstatic. You have found the original intent of all religious expression. Now your reality expands rapidly, broadening and including everything with which you come into contact.

It is here that the searcher reaches level six. Now there is a direct contact between the searcher and all that is witnessed. **The Creator** and the creature are one. Now, there is an extreme joy of expressing in whatever form that expression may take. New forms, new, enlightened expressions, are there waiting for your tongue to speak them, your fingers to write them, or your hands to paint them. You laugh at the divisions you once knew, the guilt you once felt and the being you once thought you were. You know now that death is no more than a rule of a social game and that you are continuous through all eternity.

Level seven is not an awareness that you remain at from this time forward. Since there is only **The Creative Investigative Process** continuing forever, there is no urgency or need for immediate action. This is, however, the level where primary decisions are made, where searchers are inspired to propose new social structures and where creativity originates.

Willing searchers are aware of how they arrived at level seven in the *hierarchy of awareness**. Knowing this, they may be able to return. The more times they return to this awareness, the surer the way becomes and the less fear they have of "losing their mind", moving easily from one level of consciousness to another. They are able then to go from level four where they are promoting a certain belief system to level six where they are intuitive and inspired, to level one where they hear their message as an

*see Appendix I

uninitiated beginner. This makes them very effective and persuasive.

Knowing themselves, they know those with whom they interact. Knowing their own *Defense-Control Mechanism* they do not rob others of their need for control or intimidate them into blind submission. Knowing others to be themselves, they are gentle and concerned in their direction but sure and forceful in expression of knowledge.

Less serious searchers try to enter this state of consciousness with hypnosis, meditation, throwing themselves into traumatic situations or by inducing it synthetically with drugs. The problem, here, is that they have no idea how they changed their *mental arrangement* and can only do so with the method that is familiar. Unless one develops **The Way** so that it can be called upon at any time, it is inaccessible at moments of need. Also, having no idea where one has been makes it impossible to bring that knowledge into action when the situation calls for it. Thus these seekers only find themselves away from level one or two while they are experiencing the effects of their means of "transportation". When away from that experience they operate from the same defective thinking that they always have. This is why they tend to become enslaved by the means that they use.

Many times individuals are unwilling and have no idea how they reached level seven or what level seven is. It may be that they were thrown into this state of consciousness by some traumatic experience that they could not handle in their usual reality. In this case they blame it on an external circumstance, person, place or deity, avoiding the knowledge of their own involvement in the process. Secretly they tremble, knowing what will happen to them and their social affairs if they participate in this awareness or allow their deception to become known. They ensconce it in words that they feel will be socially acceptable and strive to maintain their social identity, dropping back into level one of the *hierarchy of awareness.*

When a *Person of Knowledge* speaks, acts or expresses in some other way in the conditional world (the world of material and circumstance), the conditional world changes forever. Being the effect of creation rather than the cause of creation, it has no choice. This is why there is a great rush of creative energy when a *Person of Knowledge* is about. Acting from greatness rather than from mediocrity, a *Person of Knowledge* can change decisions that others do not even know that they have made. It is thus that *Persons of Knowledge* are capable of modifying the personal and social reality of those with whom they interact.

It is because of this that those who operate at level one in the *hierarchy of awareness* feel threatened. Since their DCM has been modified for use in the social mode, any suggestion of change in the "fundamental reality" that they have decided to embrace is met with stiff and immediate resistance. Since they are programmed to fight rather than to think, they have no choice but to react automatically to that which seems "out of place".

A *Person of Knowledge,* being them and knowing their decision and programming, does not dispute their reality but allows them to grow as they find growth possible. The greater a person becomes the more inclusive the thoughts and the less disputant the nature.

Realizations:

Knowledge, restricted and distorted for personal or social concern, becomes more and more exclusive, leaving its users frustrated, ill, confined and unfulfilled.

Knowledge, given free reign by an open mind, becomes continually more inclusive, moving from smallness, illness, fear and mediocrity, toward greatness, love, understanding and creativity.

You and I are never great alone or at the exclusion of others. Only when we learn that True Knowledge is born of being inclusive do we find the beginning of the path that leads to Greatness.

Chapter III

THE NATURE OF TRUTH
AND ITS EFFECT ON REALITY

As we witness human interaction, it soon becomes obvious that Truth is not the *mental arrangement* given to us by society in order to establish and perpetuate community. Although that lesser expression might have some characteristics that coincide with real Truth, there are many that do not. Because of this most social members have little or no ability to discern truth and must rely on the guidance of those who are in authority. This lesser "truth" becomes accepted despite the lack of provability and, in many cases, despite reason. Yet, these are the judgments with which most societies operate.

The operational "truth " of a society is usually not more than a decision to cooperate. Tenets, myths and dogmas are agreed upon by the founders as a fixative for the decisions and principles that have been chosen. In order for the society to operate, lower social members (those who have not actively participated in the selection of principles, myths and dogmas) must see these factors as true and unchallengeable. It is only in seeing beyond these shallower "truths" that Real Truth is witnessed.

In approaching Truth one does not necessarily approach that which is popular or that which is considered "good". Ideas of good and evil are social directives. Truth extends beyond social borders. It is not the province of this society or that society but is an underlying factor in the creation of all societies. To approach Truth one needs to look toward that which is the same, not that which is different. This is not the usual practice of social members. The common practice is to emphasize that which is different. Each society strives for a recognizable difference between theirs and other social groups. Here they feel that they find comfort and security.

In the search for Truth, one must be willing and prepared to step off the nicely paved highway of comfort and security into the sometimes perilous and, perhaps, materially unrewarding, forest of uncertainty. This is the point of decision. This is the place where "faith" becomes a word used and interpreted with caution, and doubt is allowed to establish a foothold. It is only when individuals doubt that which they are told to be true that they can look upon it with a discriminating eye, weighing the expression for validity, and begin to witness real Truth.

"Faith" is required to fix beliefs and hold them inviolate. Since faith is usually associated with reward or punishment it has only the limited validity that is defined by the goal to be achieved. By holding steadfast to superficial expression by use of "faith", one does not approach the depth of the expression, and Truth must remain a dim and neglected memory of who and what one really is. Those who struggle to maintain a belief system through "faith" have no faith in themselves or their ability to discern Truth.

That which must be fixed and protected from possible distruction is never Truth. The shallower the expression, the more effort must go into its care and maintenance. Then there is more conflict with the expression in the superficial world of material and circumstance. All the effort to affix that which is superficial is in vain because everything but Truth deteriorates and is eventually washed away. All promised rewards disappear as the foundations which support beliefs in separation and conflict erode and collapse under the weight of their own structure.

Truth is its own reward. It cannot be violated or destroyed. No matter how one tries to avoid, twist and distort It, Truth never changes. Only Its surface representation within the belief system appears to warp or deteriorate and must be fixed with the preservative of "faith". Truth, changeless and timeless, does not require a fixative, the approval of humankind, or the appreciation of those who benefit. The reward is in the reception and realization of Truth Itself. This and this alone is the necessary factor for the creation of a reality that is inclusive and approaches the depth of understanding that is **Universal Reality.**

One who seeks Truth is gratified by the search. All else is momentary and dispensable. While searchers may realize that they may never reach Truth, they know that they can at least approach It. (Those who can, must.) In approaching It, searchers reach down through the ever changing overburden of conflict and necessity. Suddenly they become aware that they may never be able to communicate what it is that they are finding. They press on though, in spite of the danger that no one else may understand. Even that cannot limit the search.

But what is Truth? Is it the shallow aspect of the external which may be granted or withheld? Does Truth depend on the number of believers? Or does engaging and persuading others to support our belief only popularize our error? What, then, of joining or remaining in a persuasion because of its popularity? May it not be popularized error?

In approaching Truth one can expect little help from others, for they are just as lost. Even those who are most aware can only grant words. While words may lead us to Truth, words themselves are not Truth. The quality that is Truth is much deeper than words. It is an internal awareness of what is and what is not. Truth cannot be found in the future or in the past for It stands before us, here, at this moment. Truth may be brought to our attention by many means and in a variety of languages, but that which we suddenly know has always lain there inside, waiting to be discovered. Because of the thick covering of near truth, superficial truth and social truth, Truth is fragile and elusive and must be approached on a no holds barred, catch as catch can, basis.

Yet the *Thread of Truth* runs through all expression. This is what gives the expression cohesiveness and keeps it from being self-contradictory. It is contradiction that demonstrates where a certain expression has strayed from Truth. The *Thread of Truth* is usually hidden in the overburden of the expression and is, therefore, not easily recognized.

In order to recognize the *Thread of Truth* one must see through the blanket of recitation. That which is expressed and recited is not Truth in itself but may lead the serious searcher to Truth. All expression has the limitation that words engender and is, therefore, inadequate as a means of conveying Truth. One can only lead another to the *Thread of Truth* and hope that it will be recognized and utilized.

One is either searching for the *Thread of Truth,* the rhythm and power of popular recitation, a viable explanation, or the enchantment of inexplicable mystery. Sometimes one does not even recognize or choose to be bothered with spiritual growth. It happens anyway. To choose not is to choose and spiritual growth is the result of all choices.

So it is that great persuaders of the world call our attention to great truths that approach Truth. True searchers must not only harken to their music but try to understand and be prepared, as searchers for Truth, to discard all or any part of what they now believe in the very next moment. Only then can they have an opinion worth considering and worth defending.

One of our greatest mistakes is to think that Truth is mysterious, occult or esoteric. The lesser "truths" that religious organizations surround themselves with may be, because they are purposely selected for those qualities and to proclaim a difference between themselves and other organizations. The followers are not meant to understand these "mysteries", just accept them and not question. Real Truth, however, is understandable and obvious.

Another problem is that the conscious mind is always reaching out for the spectacular and different. In doing so, it sees Truth as boring, impractical, and something that would get in the way of its projected goal. For this reason Truth may be avoided, remaining something forever taken for granted in the background of accomplishment.

Truth is the cause of reaching. Truth is in the background of all accomplishment. It is that which we have taken for granted to allow accomplishment to happen. Without Truth we would not even be capable of lying. We would not be capable of establishing lesser, limited, exclusive organizations. It is natural and obvious for all who choose to see. It is the foundation of everything we do and every thought we have. Without It there is no existence.

The measure of Truth is in the lack of self-contradiction and in the applicability of an intercepted expression to the world we are witnessing. When we realize that an expression "makes sense" and is not exclusive, we witness Truth. If we are interested in building a reality that approaches True Reality, we love the expression and change our *mental arrangement* to reflect the essence of the expression and thereby change the mode of our operation. If we are interested in retaining our *mental arrangement* unchanged upon reception of expressions that "make sense", we fear the expression and erect barriers to keep it from influencing our actions. The very experience of fear is an indication that we have intercepted an expression that has some *truth value*. When we realize the truth to which we are reacting, our *mental arrangement* changes and the fear disappears.

Because we look out from Truth, we fail to witness It; just as we cannot see our own face without a mirror. To see Truth requires reflection. Truth is the ability to paint a reality upon our mental canvas that is in concert with **The Greater Reality**. The better we arrange the paints the nearer our reality approaches **The Reality Which Knows No Barriers or Conflicts**. If, in our expression, we are creating conflicts with the expression of others and, consequently, find ourselves having to set up barriers to protect ourselves from these expressions, it is an indication that we are painting our reality badly and it is not approaching **The Greater Reality**.

This is the crux of the problem. We are so busy splashing paint upon the canvas of our memory and proclaiming it real that we are no longer aware of what Reality is. All our busy work is the result of decisions that we have made and ideas that we have given importance. Without the guidance of Truth our reality is disordered and conflicting.

To operate from Truth, we must hold in abeyance that which we have decided and consider important. This allows us to try different paints upon the canvas thereby experiencing other viewpoints. If we cannot, or are unwilling to do this because we do not trust Truth to guide us, our reality cannot change and we cannot grow in knowledge or in wisdom.

When we experience Truth, we recognize that place of

departure from others and can understand how and why they see life differently. This allows us to be more understanding and tolerant. It also allows us the possibility of growing in awareness through the interception of another viewpoint. When any fragment of the other viewpoint becomes part of the painting that we have on our canvas, we grow in knowledge and wisdom becoming greater and more inclusive. The more viewpoints we are able to intercept and include, the greater and wiser we become. It has always been our choice to either be small and narrow-minded through ignorance and exclusion of other viewpoints, remaining solely with the minimal reality we were offered in early training, or to grow in wisdom through reaching out to experience the views of others.

Our reality is the effect of the viewpoints and experiences that we encounter. When fresh paint is placed upon the canvas early in the painting due to the sudden revelation of Truth the resulting picture, though all else may be the same, changes in depth and clarity. This is the nature of our reality. As we allow ourselves to experience Truth, we are enabled and our resulting reality becomes clearer and more empowering.

Many organizations fear this because those among them who experience Truth are no longer socially reliable. Since they now see a greater reality they can no longer allow the constraints of those with lesser awareness. In an organization where this is seen as valuable, they are advanced to a higher post. In an organization where this is seen to be detrimental or threatening, they are ostracized. They still rise to great prominence in spite of the misunderstanding of others because in the background of our minds we know Truth whether we operate from It or fear It. We cannot help but give those who operate from Truth power and recognize their greatness.

In the experience of Truth, every revelation leads to a new and greater revelation just as approaching the horizon causes a new horizon. There is no place to stop and say, "Now I know everything." There is always a better way that the colors of memory and experience can be arranged upon the mental canvas.

Realizations:

You and I know what is true and what is false. Often we hide from this knowledge in order to fit in or not rock the social boat. In doing so we deprive ourselves of our personal power and a real understanding of life.

Truth stands continually before us, pounding at the door of consciousness, asking to be let in and recognized. Many, many times in our lives we have been invited to recognize it, but we are so busy with problems that we have created with superficial "truths" that we find that, even if we have the inclination, we have no time.

Our mental arrangement is always being challenged. It is only with the guidance of Truth that we are able to recognize that which enables us and that which depletes us. Once we understand this, our reality becomes coherent and we are seldom misled.

Chapter IV

STAGES OF INDIVIDUATED
HUMAN CONSCIOUSNESS*

In order to fully investigate how and why we know what we think we know, we must look closely at family and society's role in our earliest decisions. Without taking into account their effect on our lives we have little or no ability to estimate that which we have personally decided or that which we have been invited to decide by others. We are, therefore, powerless to decide what we can and cannot change without disrupting those with whom we interact. We are equally powerless to recognize what we must change if we are to creatively use our talents and experience a satisfying and rewarding life. Without such an analysis, many, if not most, of us are doomed to be frustrated, overstressed and unfulfilled.

The first question that needs to enter our mind in order to initiate the process of investigation is, "What or who am I?" Without this question there is no personal investigation. There are many people who will tell you who and what you are. They will say that you are John Jones, Mary Smith or whatever the social name is that they have given you and recorded in the social archives. They will say that you are a hairdresser, a dentist, a writer, or whatever the social position or occupation is that you hold. They will tell you where you work, what your marital status is, where you live, perhaps even what your habits are. By doing this, they seek to identify you as different and separate from all other life forms.

You are much more than can be categorized and identified socially. You are the ability to categorize and identify. To know who and what we really are we need

*see Appendix II

31

only examine our own subconscious processes. Here there is much that is obvious, yet it is completely overlooked and taken for granted.

All bodily motions, chemistry and thought behavior is ignored as being obvious and much less than unusual. Still, the digestion of food requires more knowledge than any conscious activity we may undertake. Our consciousness exists with permission of our subconscious. The amount of knowledge in the subconscious realm which allows human consciousness to exist is infinitely greater.

Usually, the social consideration of the subconscious is that it is a pit where we rid ourselves of conscious problems. From this area, it is said that demons of our past come to haunt our present. Many of us are reluctant to give credence to the idea that there is such a thing as the subconscious mind. When we do acknowledge this "lower" mental process, it is with deprecation, as though it were something separate from us and less than human.

Now that science has given us a look at some of our subconscious occurrences, we begin to appreciate this inner knowledge that we use but are not conscious of using. Heart, breath, temperature control, and all bodily functions are intricate and integrated. One cell of the human body is so complicated that human consciousness is only now beginning to appreciate its complexity. Yet that single cell is but a minute part of our subconscious mind which we so arrogantly dismiss as "lower". This is a conflict within ourselves, the pretense that part of what we are is better than other parts of what we are.

We want to believe that the conscious controls the subconscious. Yet, there is no real separation between these mental facilities. Therefore, whatever is in control, it is still us doing the controlling. How can human consciousness be separate from that which gives it existence and supports it? Why do we believe that there is such a separation?

In looking outwardly, away from ourselves, we ignore and take for granted that which we really are and see ourselves as we appear externally, to others. We measure ourselves through their eyes and see ourselves as we fit or do not fit into their world.

In failing to know ourselves, we cannot know, accurately, anything else. In taking for granted the *yardstick* with which we measure the world, we measure blindly and haphazardly. The same characteristic takes on a different color for each individual since it is concocted and compounded by the conscious mind, measured poorly and filed indiscriminately. Because we take for granted that we are doing this properly, we are frustrated and confused by a world that does not support our beliefs. When this happens we try to change the world.

A prime factor in knowing ourselves and how we measure the world is knowing how we came to be as we are. As we recognize fault in our vision, we are better able to modify our thinking and overcome distortions we create in our reality. As this happens, the reality we create approaches the reality that we witness and conflict disappears.

As was mentioned previously, our reality is continually changing. We do not have the reality that we were born with or the reality we experienced as a small child. Neither our personal reality nor the world of circumstance is the same from one moment to the next.

If we are to recognize and accept this, we must recognize and accept the process of evolution. This is paramount to our continued development. To believe that nothing evolves or develops is tantamount to saying that you are exactly the same as you were as a child with the same thoughts and the same ambitions. (If this is the case, then you probably are not evolving and this entire treatise has no significance in your reality.) Only those who can recognize and appreciate the evolution of other creatures and of consciousness as a whole can recognize and appreciate their own mental evolution.

Consider the slowly rising animal consciousness as evolutionary processes approach human faculties. The continual looking toward the external for protection and survival would cause a disregard for internal functions and thought processes. Also, search, interest and adventure would be continually outward and never inward. Thought and memory, while present, would never enter conscious awareness. Consciousness would only entertain forms, sounds, smells, etc. sensed from the external. Since events and accomplishments leading to this state of consciousness had already been experienced, they would be regarded as already known and, therefore, not interesting. There would be no reason for the prehuman being to look inwardly at its own mental process.

That which distinguishes human from other animal life is not the ability to "think". The ability to recognize and organize, arriving at the more complex which we term thought is contained to greater or lesser degree in all existence. The distinguishing feature of humanity is the desire and need to recognize thought processes.

The more evolved animals have the ability and tendency to become attached to the remembered and, therefore, the inability to accept drastic change without emotional pain. It is through reflection that we are able to modify our beliefs and change reaction to the world of material and circumstance. Without such reflection we are as powerless in controlling the conditional world as any other animal. With reflection, we witness new ways to think and act when confronted with a certain circumstance. This frees us from emotional slavery.

As human consciousness comes into existence it has a cautionary tag which says, "This facet of Universal Consciousness is incomplete." It is this that is recognized and expressed by religions. Their primary function is to bring this transition to its completion by causing participants to understand their involvement in Universal Process. Unfortunately, few religions know their primary function.

The "unfinished tag" is necessary due chiefly to the concentration of the evolving mind on external material and circumstance. All of the evolutionary developments and achievements promoting this stage are relegated to the known and taken for granted in the outward striving toward the external and new.

In the more evolved animal there is a sensual awareness and memory, but these factors are completely controlled by the subconscious or unconscious mind except for the aforementioned tendency of attachment to the remembered, a rudimentary human consciousness.

As the non-verbal consciousness expands with external communications, first in the form of motions, noises and later language, it begins to consider itself separate, as though it exists in and for itself. A gradual shift develops from reliance on the subconscious, internal, intuitive toward reliance on the conscious and external.

Every child, as it develops, must go through this evolutionary process. In approaching human birth we experience all stages of development from crystalline structure, to one-celled flagellate and one-celled ovum, to conceived protozoa, to swimming organism, to parasitic growth, to reptilian intelligence, to basic mammal, to primate, and finally to human intelligence. The neglect of any step of this development would leave an insurmountable void, destroying the possibility of human existence.

(The same holds true for the experiences that lead to Knowledge and Greatness. Neglect or ignorance of any step leaves the searcher incomplete and inadequate. Only by being inclusive of all viewpoints encountered does one enter this realm. Any exclusion or neglect robs one of the necessary insight.)

With ever increasing interplay between memory and senses, the human conscious realm grows. Though it is insignificant in comparison to the knowledge within the subconscious realm and not really separate, consciousness develops the tendency to remember itself as separate, apart, and different. The illusory separation is a programmed error rising from our externally oriented past. Prior to birth, as an embryo, there is no separation, only Unity of Being. Man and woman, sperm and egg, together, combined, just as the thumb and forefinger of a hand are brought together with purpose and intention, so it is that Universal Mind weaves the substance of Self. What is necessary is known, as are how and why. The action and the substance are proof of knowledge, moving at the will of Universal Mind. Mind logs performance values into memory. Pulse and organ functions are carefully monitored and recorded. Mind analyzes and corrects defects in all systems including the maternal body which Mind attempts to impress to conscious awareness and control more directly than when in a non-pregnant condition.

To aid you in the recognition of the growth of your own consciousness, human life, from birth to death has been divided into ten stages. These divisions are arbitrary and are not meant to be exact statements of your or anyone else's personal development. You are the ultimate knower of how you developed and what decisions you made along the way. The purpose, here, is to bring that knowledge, which you now take for granted, to your conscious attention. This explanation is idealized and no attempt has been made to make it conform with the views of modern psychology or your personal belief.

FIRST STAGE: At birth the consciousness of a child does not yet know separation. The child is part of and involved in all that brought it into existence. Approaching the final automatic stages of evolutionary development, the child begins experiencing sensual awareness. Temperature differences, light variations, sounds and odors begin to enter the conscious awareness. These differences become classified in importance and logged into memory. There are basic decisions made here about what is usual and what is rare, about what is welcomed, what is acceptable, and what is unwelcome and unacceptable. From these fragments of information, the child constructs an initial reality.

At this point, the child is at the first stage of human consciousness. An awareness of very basic differences has been formed. The child has created a reality that suffices to fill its infant needs. That which is rare and momentary is neglected, while that which is repeated becomes familiar and significant. Every child makes a slightly different arrangement of these initial impressions depending on the inner urgings that call the child to classify and make arrangements.

Life for the newborn is very much like running a maze. There is nothing to tell you what is a right or wrong decision in your classifying and arranging of impressions. There is no way to know what decision will be enabling or which will be depleting. It is as though you are faced with a path that is walled with brick; you come to a fork in the path and you must make a decision now. There is no time to dawdle and gather more information and the remainder of your life will be based on these momentary decisions.

Having once decided, you know that there will be no turning back. You will only be faced with new circumstances and new decisions that must be made. If you are lucky and arrange your sense impressions well, you will grow in knowledge and awareness, and be happy and fulfilled. If not, you will become frustrated, embitterred and ill-tempered. But, of course, you do not know this at the time. (This doesn't mean that these decisions and your consequent mental arrangement cannot be changed later.)

In the infant, Mind strives to maintain greater complexity. It continues committing to memory actions and movements. There is still no conscious thought of life, death, or separation. Mind looks upon the external with infant eyes and hears with infant ears. The external aspect, manifest in the father and mother, welcomes the internal aspect's complexification. The consciousness of the parents sees only the external but there is an underlying awareness of **Non-separation and Universal Continuum** present in all actions. The first two years of this facet of Mind are spent in recording movement and external aspects. All actions are the result of these early decisions.

SECOND STAGE: Mind logs into the memory of the child that which is controlled by the child's actions and that which controls the child's actions. Mind also records that which appears neutral. The early decisions of separation begin here as Mind logs into memory more external aspects. With the commencement of language memorization, controlling, non-controlling and controlled by, goes toward "me or not me", "mine or not mine".

Concepts of separation and individuation are slowly introduced and learned by the young consciousness. These concepts are necessary for the maintainence of the greater mental order and to express the creative process in the external, conditional world. Before this time, the child's personality and separation exist only in the parent mind. Now,

because Mind has relegated everything previously commit-
ted to memory to the customary and usual, Mind looks
outward absorbed in the unusual and different. In doing
so, the child intellect moves from the Totality toward conscious mental distinction and separation.

THIRD STAGE: Each new memory becomes a tool
to further creative process and the cause for further division. The child is now walking, talking and interacting with
older brothers and sisters, parents or relatives. The me,
you, and them relationship grows. Each new word adds to
the sense of separation.

An awareness grows in memory, too, of the fuss "others" are making, whether there is acceptance, rejection,
annoyance or enjoyment. These are logged in the control-
controlled categories. The complicated memory system of
human consciousness shifts from control to ownership.
The consciousness begins to test all external aspects to see
what is owned. This includes relatives, parents, acquain-
tances and other external aspects. All this information becomes part of the growing child's reality. The sense of
separation now begins to cause frustration and disappointment when what is now owned does not compare favora-
bly with the memory of what was previously owned, or
what is owned by "others."

FOURTH STAGE: The youth is now of school age.
In elementary school the child recognizes ownership of
personality, physical image (mostly facial but body shape
and size also), relative intelligence, physical abilities, sex,
parental financial status, social class, race and religion.
Human mind separates more and more from Universal
Mind. In looking continually outward it becomes more lost
in memory as each recognized difference becomes a
wedge separating the Total Self and the conscious, remembered, external self of the conditional world.

Recognition of individuality and fear of death further separate the conscious and what is now seen as the "subconscious". It is during this time, too, that separation from other planetary life such as plants and animals occurs as the child learns the name of each and is taught its difference. Some individuals separate farther and faster than others, while some barely recognize or fail to recognize the separation. The degree and speed of separation depends on the amount of importance that the conscious mind attaches to each remembered aspect.

FIFTH STAGE: Even though there is much separation by the time the youngster approaches high school, there is still a great amount of spiritual or Mind control present. While external factors have great influence, the major control is still intuitive. Most of the ideas that bring about separation are present but have not yet completely solidified. There is, in most cases, the tendency to fight external control and defy authority. Mind must gauge that which is being seen now against the backdrop of what it has seen. (Each generation brings a new challenge and presently "new" Mind with "now" memories cannot be restrained by yesterday.)

SIXTH STAGE: Separation, by now, has approached near maximum. The young adult feels alone, abandoned and separated as early friends go their own way. The person is no longer involved in family and completely absorbed in individuation. Or the person might cling to family and a few friends to avoid feeling alone. Although the human consciousness is still compelled by Mind, there is no conscious awareness of Union. In looking outward, the sense of ownership, competition, and the desire to prove and improve image increase the sense of separation from the Total Mind.

SEVENTH STAGE: Joining in relationships, affairs, small groups, and/or marriage, the individual gives up some separation. The adult now realizes attachments in the external but these are offset by additional competition and responsibility. The desire to prove oneself professionally and socially is strong. Family or group growth adds to attachments, but these are usually selfish, external bonds similar to ownership. The errors and concerns of youth fade away, but new errors and concerns for acceptance take their place.

EIGHTH STAGE: The individual finds meaning in work and group activities, joins clubs, participates in sports, and becomes an organization member. There is a lessening of the feeling of being by oneself and the beginning of a sense of being involved in something greater. It is at this stage that the individual volunteers for community activities, helps at social gatherings and seeks fulfillment in doing "worthwhile deeds". Being involved in the greater self of organization and country, the person is no longer alone or totally separate. Now there is meaning and purpose, a reason for living.

NINTH STAGE: Upon retirement and family growth, the individual loses many causes of separation. If the adult can relinquish the sense of responsibility for family, the condition of the world, and can pierce the cluttered shallows of religion, Truth begins to dawn.

Any sense of ownership, responsibility, or failure causes the separation to be maintained. Differences that once seemed so important and continued the sense of separation can now melt, if allowed, as one moves toward complete union. Trying to retain the past is trying to retain the division between the conscious and the subconscious; between Mind, the rememberer, and person, the remembrance. Fear of death and concern about the "hereafter" are a final memory that human consciousness must erase to transcend the error that separation is real.

TENTH STAGE: In "death" Union is complete. Ideas of separation gained during "life" dissolve and Mind is All, undifferentiated. But, then, Mind was never separate. All of those separating ideas gathered and nourished during "life", personality, individuality, sex, ownership, indebtedness, wealth, ambition, sense of failure or accomplishment, all responsibility, concern for family and friends, and millions of other bits and pieces gained during the human form that separated you, the human, from **You, The Universe,** all fade into irrelevance. Through "death" of your attachment to the superficial and conditional, you recognize your union with **That Which is Eternal.**

This need not happen when the body, gasping for its final breath, loses its ability to sustain the separated remembered self. It can happen at any time, for the conscious mind is never really separate. It is only the shadows of Mind's memory, coming and going as creative process demands. It is only the pretense of consciousness to be separate that gives rise to the perpetuation of the remembered self and the "life" of the person. When the pretense is not sustained, The Creator reigns, immortal and supreme; and love, peace, joy and harmony abound. Mind recognizing Itself releases all judgment and the world begins anew. This can happen at anytime, even now.

Realizations:

What you and I think we are is the product of our development. Our realities are the result of our early training and experience. Every action we take is the effect of the reality that you or I have personally generated. As we learn to generate truth and become inclusive in our thoughts we approach greater understanding and the pleasure of participation in Infinite Process.

Mind strives for consciousness of Self within the human lifespan. To attain this, it must take the human consciousness through many lessons. Some of these lessons are fearful and unpleasant to human consciousness because of its attachment to body in the world of material and circumstance.

The speed at which you and I wish to progress spiritually is our decision. One thing is certain, even if we try to avoid spiritual growth, we will leave this lifespan with a greater awareness than we had when we entered. Whether the journey is difficult or pleasant is up to us.

We may, if we wish, hang on to our conflicted beliefs and experience the bitterness, frustration and disappointment that attends errors of perception or we may embrace Truth and allow all conflict and error to be resolved. Now, in this moment, we are The Creator in action. The world is as we are choosing it to be.

Chapter V

PARTICIPATORY LEVELS OF CONSCIOUSNESS*

All divisions made in Consciousness are arbitrary. Being so, they do not adhere to absolute formulation but rather to the will and purposes of the divider. Since all individualized consciousness divides differently **That Which Is Ultimately Indivisible**, these divisions seem to be real and are proclaimed so by the decision of the participating individuated aspects of consciousness adjoined in agreement.

Common reality is, therefore, not so much an absolute as it is a fabrication of all the bits and pieces of Reality that the human aspect of Mind encounters and agrees to hold intact for social purposes. While individualized aspects of human consciousness may tend to disagree, they recognize the social benefits of operation from a common point of agreement.

As has been indicated in Stages of Human Consciousness, the individuation of reality or personal *mental arrangement* is the result of decisions and reactions in the conditional world. As such it has no relationship to Reality which is **The Indivisible Union of All Manifestation.**

Since all individuation is arbitrary, the *participatory levels of consciousness* offered here are also. As has been mentioned, these levels, as all individuations, are decided and held to be "true" by agreement of consciousness. That does not make this expression less true or more true than other expressions. It does, however, assure an equality of expression that allows consciousness to decide the merit and value applicable.

What is offered here is a map of individuation from total separation, through various levels of awareness, to

*see Appendix III

Total Union. In this study, each level has *creatively effective characteristics* and *creatively defective characteristics*. Making a distinction between effective and defective is not meant to imply that there is some "right" or "wrong" way to be.

Being is Self-justified and, therefore, unjudgeable, as are all acts of Mind. Judgment is the result of decision and subsequent agreement within the human aspect of consciousness. When the suggested division is made and *effective creativity* is decided and agreed "right", a pattern to be followed, its counterpart *defective creativity* becomes "wrong", a pattern to be avoided.

All occurrences are as the **Consciousness of the Universe** decides through the operation of all Its aspects. It is through the human aspect of Consciousness that the decision to be *creatively effective* or *creatively defective* is declared and maintained.** Through this aspect and no other is this decision relevant.

The condition of separation is analogous to being in a *canyon of conceit**. Here the decision of Mind, acting through the aspect of human consciousness, is to consider Itself as separate. In doing so, It narrows Its focus with decisions of difference and comparative value. From this *canyon*, vision is obscured as the opening, limited by differences and comparative importances, defines the area of Reality that can be viewed. The rest remains obscured until separated consciousness acts from a higher plane within this *canyon*.

Level One:
TOTAL ISOLATION AND DETACHMENT

Creatively Effective Characteristics:
Swift, unrestricted action. Ability to accomplish

* see Appendix IV
** see Appendix VIII

great feats without concern for body, society, family or others. This is the height of extension where Mind knows only the feat to be performed through human consciousness. This is the province of the limit finder and the saint. Here there is no concern with life and death, only performance.

Here, there is complete detachment from any influence with absolute and total concentration on the act of being and doing. This arrangement is set by the development of concentration and released by deciding the importance of any one object or objective over any other object or objective.

Creatively Defective Characteristics:

Psychosis. Paranoia. Deformation or destruction of the body. Terror of what is seen as other; sometimes this is the body. Disease through not paying attention to physical demands of the body. Anger and ill temper with all aspects of Self, since the aspect discussed sees all aspects separate. This is the province of the psychopath and the madman.

Here there is a detachment from all that is not self but still protecting a self that it sees as non-existent from the attack of other possible selves. Human consciousness, not recognizing its attachment even to body, and seeing itself completely separate from all that it encounters, considers itself either superior or inferior, either proud or fearful. To the degree it makes these distinctions important it acts violent or catatonic to stimuli it encounters.

This arrangement is set by realizing only the action that is taking place and becoming totally involved in that action. It is released by attachment of importance to some more inclusive aspect of consciousness.

*　　*　　*

This is the deepest level within the *canyon of conceit**. Mind, in allowing the greatest extreme of separation, does so with caution. This aspect of Mind within the realm of human consciousness is always counterbalanced with other aspects for direction and support.

The separated aspect may see itself as completely separate and independent in its action and of its action. All the while, the action is totally supported by Mind. Supporting aspects of human consciousness are prepared to overlook this condition. Subtly, they are able to redirect the separated aspect which, in itself, has no real ability to decide and, therefore, no ability to direct itself.

Aspects which do not see beyond surface condition, their own fears and their own insecurities, but rather condemn what they see as "a person gone astray," are not supportive and their direction is not considered by Mind acting through the aspect of the separated self except as an irritant and stimulus for negative reaction.

To operate at this level, the aspect of Mind must have acquired a fixation or obsession that requires total attention. As soon as something else begins to matter, consciousness cannot maintain the level of concentration necessary to sustain operation.

Being narrow of purpose, separated consciousness has very limited vision. At he bottom of the *canyon of conceit,* consciousness can only see that which it has chosen to do in spite of all consequences or restrictions. Only when this action is either carried out or the obsession is broken by the supporting aspect can the totally separated consciousness be redirected.

Most operation at this level is episodic as attention is

*see Appendix IV

brought back to bodily needs or to a greater level of consciousness for redirection. In the most *effectively creative* combinations, the supportive aspect of consciousness, whether within the same body, another body or group of bodies, knows the ultimate dangers of *defective creation* and is able to cause something other than the obsession to matter when applicable. This action breaks the fixation and causes the necessity of redirection.

Level Two:
THE SEPARATED INDIVIDUAL

Creatively Effective Characteristics:

Single-mindedness. Able to personally extend through competition, tone body muscles and mental facilities for best performance. Not restrained by opinion or regulation except where it is life threatening. (This can be overruled by greater threat.)

Identification with the body and bodily processes. Recognition and acceptance of external motivating factors such as awards, monetary remuneration, respect of peers and the applause of masters. Aspect sees itself as capable and prides itself in individual excellence.

This arrangement is set by realizing only individual performance. It is released by realizing team or family effort.

Creatively Defective Characteristics:

Neurosis. Loneliness. Depression. Thinking itself always right while everyone else is wrong or vice versa. Battling with those whose opinions differ. Anxieties of condition, image and time. Illness due to the belief in fault and guilt. Overconcern with memory and aging. Mistakes of real and ideal.

Aspect sees itself as superior, inferior or oscillates between these ideas of self. It looks for others to consider itself better or worse. Always unsatisfied and unfulfilled. Victim or oppressor of the world that is witnessed.

This arrangement is set by making comparison of self to others important. It is released by relaxing this idea of self importance.

* * *

This is the deepest level one may reach in the *canyon of conceit** and still remain intelligible and communicative. This is the level of neurosis. Here, individuated human consciousness sees only bodily desires and separation. Looking up from near the bottom of this *canyon* vision is narrowed and exclusive. There is only an individualized consciousness in competition with all that it sees. It seeks fame, wealth and power, feeling that it needs to get ahead and stay ahead of others like itself.

Here, competition is strong. Honed by Mind, individualized aspects are prepared to vie for awards of recognition and power by organizers within the system. Since there is very limited ability to decide effectively at this level, trained and controlled individual aspects of human consciousness can achieve success in the hands of a good organizer.

This is a level of vanity where there is a constant concern for appearance or "what others might think." This is a handle they give others on control of their actions all the while they consider themselves free and independent. Organizers recognize and use whatever means they encounter to achieve control.

There are many individuals at this level who are crea-

*see Appendix IV

tively defective. They have no ability to cooperate, believing all the while that they are right, completely alone and victimized by the world they witness. Their world is fixed. They are the ones who "know" while no one else "understands". They feel beset and beleaguered as they confront and do battle with others who are obviously in error.

This is a trap that extenders* can easily fall into as they introduce a new concept to the world they witness. Usually the social world is composed chiefly of maintainers* and so cannot hear or witness a viewpoint that is not approved by their organizer*.

Organizers*, on the other hand, are seldom at this level and even then, only briefly. They do, however, understanding desires and fears, know how to handle those who operate at this level.

Maintainers* arrive at this level in carrying out the directives and proclaiming the absolutism of the belief given to them by their organizers*. Seeing themselves totally responsible for its dissemination, they feel that no one is more aware than they are of the consequences of actions that they do not see as proper.

Mind acts through sponsors and supporters to direct the action at this level since self direction is usually ineffective and muddled. The support and direction may come from a higher level of consciousness within the same body, a higher level of consciousness within another body or within a group of bodies. Wherever the support comes from, it is always Mind.

* These distinctions are further detailed in Chapter VI, on page 67.

Level Three:
FAMILY

Creatively Effective Characteristics:

Cooperation. With others like itself the individuated human aspect of consciousness finds greater ability to accomplish. Interception and interaction enhance the creative process. Common language enhances communications. Encouragement promotes success.

Each family member is enhanced by each other family member. The action of Mind is multiplied through the agreement of members.

This arrangment is set by recognizing differences between family of participation and other families, and making these differences important. It is released by realizing that participation at the family level is by agreement and that basicallly all families have similar problems.

Creatively Defective Characteristics:

Fixed-mindedness. Concern for family image. Infighting and antipathy. Lack of purpose. Superiority to or fear of other families, or those who look, speak or act differently. Gossipmongery. Feudery. Unreasonable ownership.

This arrangement is set by making family differences important and seeing other families as faulted or offensive. It is released by realizing familial similarities.

* * *

No matter how separate and distinct an aspect of consciousness is, there are always others who think and act similarly or in a way that augments and is enhancing. In choosing to look for those others, separated consciousness approaches the family level of consciousness. Usually, this level is automatic as the individual accepts the biological family. Sometimes it is more difficult as the individual has a sense of not belonging.

In finding others like oneself, one loses a certain amount of aloneness. Here, there is a sense of being part of something greater and more inclusive. Now, the interaction of individuals becomes more than each individual was separately. In this level of operation is a distinct language that is not common to other families but testifies to the common experience of family members. It also testifies to their uncommonness with other families.

This commonness the members experience is not necessarily peaceful or understanding. It can be explosive and violent. Family members may only get together to argue and rail at one another. With no external input, alternative possibilities of behavior may not exist. Families accept the mode in which they operate. Even though it may be a very difficult behavior pattern, it is familiar; therefore, it is comfortable for those who participate.

There is much creative energy at this level of operation. The individuals can have set minds and set purposes as they cooperate with one another to extend their individual abilities. When operating in concert at the family level of consciousness, individuality, in fact, ceases to exist and each participant knows their involvement in total achievement.

When out of concert or discordant, each member experiences the need for accord. This is what makes true family action. Each member has the possibility of bringing about accord. Each member has the possibility of rejecting the accord. A family is a family because it chooses to be and for no other reason. When the accord is broken the family ceases to exist except as a hunger, the need for accord.

Individuals operative at this level try to find family or cause family to happen. Other individuals they meet are measured for possible familial relationship. If the others appear acceptable in other matters, the one concerned with familial relationship tries to establish accord. If accord cannot be established a pretended familial relationship is detrimental to both parties, keeping both from approaching a relationship where accord is evident.

Many *creatively defective* relationships happen as participants use ideas of fault, blame and guilt to bring about and maintain a familial relationship. This action is destructive of accord and results in false family operation.

Another method of creating familial relationship is through tacit, oral or written agreement. This always works if there is accord. Where it is absent, such agreements tend to fall apart, leaving the participants disappointed and angry. An expressed agreement is only a shadow of the accord that brings it into existence. Accord cannot be expressed or controlled by agreement.

Level Four:
ORGANIZATION

Creatively Effective Characteristics:
Regulation. Common policy and rules allow cooperation between large number of members. Members are freed from making major decisions giving them greater freedom to act (within guidelines). Due to free and unrestricted exchange of ideas and opinions all members are enhanced by growth of membership.

Amiable competition with other organizations. Open and free acceptance of members who are in accord with stated principles. Enhancement of life external to the organization.

This arrangement is set by agreement to dogmas, creeds or tenets and rules of conduct. It is released by disagreement.

Creatively Defective Characteristics:

Restriction. Fear of loss of membership. Fear of loss of other members. Overgrowth. Poor leadership. Conflict with other organizations.

This arrangement is set by organizational control through use of fear and mystery to dominate members. It is released through member realization of inner strength and knowledge.

* * *

In any organization there are a number of families. The organizational level is more inclusive and though these families may disagree with one another, they may be in firm agreement on the principles set forth by their organization. It is knowing this accord to be greater than their familial differences that brings them together in common purpose at the organizational level.

Part of the function of the organization is to help individuals find familial accord. In doing so, the organization grounds itself at the family level, enabling both the family and the organization. Organizations that pay no attention to familial relationships soon lose their ability to sustain membership. This membership is eroded by organizations that pay attention to the family level of consciousness.

In an operative organization, strong accord between members causes rules and agreements that enhance the creativity of members at the individual level of consciousness. In enabling its individual members, the organization enables itself.

The organizational consciousness is inclusive of all individual members and all familial relationships. Not considering lesser individuations important, organizers apply themselves at the organizational level, making important only the difference between their own and other's organizations.

Here organizers act as clergy, expressing dogma, heeding to tenets or creeds, and urging maintainers to do likewise. Control is lodged in the ability to "handle" the maintainers, giving them applause, appreciation, recognition and awards of merit for their performance. Maintainers, seeing themselves as small, insignificant and needing approval, are easily lead into doing the will of the organizer.

Extenders who are organizers operate intermittently at this level to enable and empower those who have the desire and willingness to realize inclusiveness rather than separation. Since there is no desire on their part to maintain an extending organization they do not make the decisions that organizational maintenance requires. Consequently, when there is no longer a need or requirement for what they have to offer, the organization usually disbands.

Level Five:
NATIONAL

Creatively Effective Characteristics:
Ability to bring great numbers of individuals, families and organizations together for massive proj-

ects. Establishment of law allowing participants greater participation in the larger body. (Many characteristics here are the same as the organizational characteristics, except on a greater scale.)

Promotion of trade and amiable competition with other national bodies. Development of common enterprise and reciprocal agreements.

This arrangement is set by realizing national or common language interests. It is released by concerns of private interest.

Creatively Defective Characteristics:

Restriction. Fear of loss of citizenry. Fear of being taken over by other system. Isolationism. Poor leadership. Belief that only one nation's economic system is viable. Fear of other nations. Overpopulation. Terrorism.

This arrangement is set by ignoring all but national interest of those participating in common language and expression. It is released by recognizing national interest of other language and expression.

* * *

Consciousness at the national level is similar to that at the organizational level. Here, though, the divisions are based, not on creed primarily, but on language and geographical location. Just as organization is inclusive of large numbers of families and individuals, so nation is inclusive of a large number of organizations, families and individuals.

This is the province of patriots as individuals act from national purpose. This division they hold important. All lesser divisions are minor and inconsequential. They devote their lives and their talents toward making their nation the best it can be, often giving up their lives in the process. Knowing the inclusiveness of their decisions they willingly risk death to create and sustain national interests. They know the smaller division of their personal life to be much, much less than that of their national life.

At one extreme those at this level of consciousness are peacemakers and enablers aiding other nations as they aid their own. At the other extreme, they are guerrillas and terrorists, determined to have their right to self-determination and independence recognized by other nations.

Level Six:
HUMANITY

Creatively Effective Characteristics:
Great release of talent and creativity through the human aspect of Mind. Ability to appreciate all human endeavors and act from knowledge of combined human ability. Broadened understanding and heightened awareness. Recognition that conflict is a part of creative process. Inclusiveness in all acts.

Creatively Defective Characteristics:
Inability to decide and act. Avoidance of human enterprise. Blaming humanity for what is perceived as faults. Distruction of humanity for the "good" of humanity. Praying for peace (except personal). Efforts to unite humanity (as it is already united). Conflict with that which is seen as non-human.

* * *

With the inclusion of all nations and all subsequent divisions, there are no opposing forces in human consciousness. Now, does this aspect of mind function at the will of human concern rather than the will of national concern, or some lesser concern. Now, everything in lower levels of consciousness is taken into consideration.

The extremes of this level of consciousness are humanity in concert with other animal forms and nature, and humanity in conflict with other animal forms and nature. Effectivity or defectivity follows from this initiating decision upon the division of humanity from other aspects of Mind.

The creativity that follows from these decisions is similarly effected and unfolds in either concert or in conflict. Extenders operate best in this realm, recognizing that which causes in-concert-creation to happen and applying their talents to direct the creation effectively.

This is also the realm of the Metaphysical philosopher. Acting as a medium between Mind and the aspect of Mind known as humanity, this extender enables aspects at lesser levels by bringing deeper truths to conscious attention. By doing so, new ways to organize happen and **The Creation** is enhanced.

Inasmuch as operation at this level of consciousness requires the free flow of ideas and insight, only extenders and extender-enablers exist at this level. Consciousness, here, is ultimately organized and has no requirement for organizers. Only at lower levels of consciousness are organizers effective. Maintainers also do not reach this level of consciousness for the previously stated reason.

Level Seven:
ANIMAL

Effective and defective creation are meaningless concepts at this level of consciousness as control by Mind is more direct. Here, that aspect of mind that is creature consciousness has no ability to make anything more than judgments of necessity and adventure. There is no conscious recognition of The Creation nor the possibility of recognizing purpose.

Creature consciousness can only act and react to circumstances. There is, however, investigation and the ability to classify, but extension is limited by a lessened amount of permission. Here, awareness is lodged in Mind as It extends through creature consciousness.

This is the realm of *Spiritually Communicative Consciousness.* Not knowing Its separation from **The Source of Being,** It expresses the union of all creatures through sounds and actions, encouraging aspects of consciousness at lesser levels to know This Union.

Level Eight:
LIVING

As at the animal level, the effectivity or ineffectivity of creation is not a factor. At this juncture of what is seen to human consciousness as life and death, there is only the continuation of beingness and growingness. While life has importance it is not more important than **The Creative Process** that brings it into existence and sustains it.

This is the realm of the *Spiritually Non-communicative.* Here, there is no need to explain or encourage. There is just being and happening. Every sight brings new understanding and every sound a new expression of life.

Level Nine:
UNIVERSAL OR COSMIC

Now, there is no division between that which is seen as living and non-living by lesser consciousness. This is where all division ceases and **The Total Union of Existence** is recognized.

The human aspect of consciousness may only encounter this once in a "moment of truth", a "holy instant", a "religious experience", "the peace that surpasses all understanding", **Unconditional Love or The Realization of Union.** Having encountered this awareness all subsequent divisions are reformed and consciousness moves up into a more aware position within the *canyon of conceit.*

This is the province of **Undifferentiated Spirit,** nameless and incomparable, **Total Awareness*.** All else is born of decisions of division and separation. Being smaller than **The Totality of Existence,** less inclusive aspects are subject to the circumstances that are prevalent and decided within the level of consciousness chosen.

Realizations:

You may be called to operate at a certain level of consciousness while I am called to operate from another. To praise or ridicule either of us is to praise or ridicule Mind, of which we are an aspect.

Communication between aspects of consciousness operating at different levels is difficult. Each level has its own language, and each aspect its own motivation.

Most effective operation in the world of material and circumstance happens at the organizational level because this level has the greatest concentration of human consciousness.

Everyone operates at all levels of consciousness but there is a certain level to which we feel a greater attraction. When we operate at the level of our calling everything seems to work out and we experience the joy of being really alive.

*see Appendix IV

Chapter VI

SEASONS OF HUMAN DEVELOPMENT*

As is the case with the individual human in the life journey, from completeness, through separation, back to completeness, so it is that humanity is destined to travel from initiation to completion. As the greater knowledge of the subconscious is translated to human consciousness, new seasons unfold with new problems and new ideas. With the solving of each problem, another passage in the maze of human intellect is conquered. The way is long and arduous. Finally we are Complete, Whole and United just as we were in the beginning before the translation began. Once more we are in Union with **The Totality of Being**, but now we are aware and conscious of The Union.

As with the Stages of Human Consciousness, so too, the Seasons of Human Development offered here are arbitrary and may be affixed in some other manner in another expression. The object is to offer you an overview so that you may better understand your own operational decisions and the operational decisions of those with whom you interact in the time period of your experience. Mind, which is **The Ultimate Decision Maker**, knows best what your function is and how you are to fulfill your life's purpose.

If this differs from the belief you now hold in memory, you can either cling to that belief, perhaps holding this suggestion in ridicule, accept parts as true and parts as false, hold this suggestion in abeyance, modify your belief to be inclusive of this possibility, or abandon your belief because this suggestion is more applicable to the circumstances you have encountered. The choice is yours. You **are** the arranger of your reality.

*see Appendix V

One place we can agree, though (provided that we are looking for a place of agreement), as humans we did not know in infancy what we know now. And in the next five minutes we will be more aware than we are at present. This is a truth we can all witness. If we choose we can recognize that this is the circumstance of The Creation. As we extend, It extends, for It extends through our thoughts and actions (and through the thoughts and actions of other creatures as well).

FIRST SEASON: In the dawning humanity there is an acceptance of life and a survival consciousness. As yet, there is no awareness of death. The creatures, extending through creative process, have a relatively short term memory from which to draw. As a result there is little concern. They eat and sleep where and when possible, establishing and defending territories to maintain the food supply and stabilize living conditions.

As Mind moves to greater complexification, so does the animal consciousness which is Mind evolution approaching human form. This movement, this change, this development, is not without concern as Mind moves toward a new dimension of Self, the reflection of Its own extension.

Mind now acts within the new dimension to establish the memory of Itself even as It extends, translating the familiar into a new language abounding with possibility. Minds warns Itself in the new form that it is unfinished. There is much translation that will only happen with time (an element logged into consciousness to stimulate creation), but eventually this aspect will have complete awareness of its possibility and purpose. Until then, it must tag that which it does not yet understand with the realization that there is a Greater Self that knows the how and why of all things.

From its earliest experience, the lesser self which is the extension in the new dimension recognizes and honors the Greater Self in which it is involved. Knowing no separation, the lesser self experiences no fear and is completely in harmony with the world of material and circumstance, the reality it witnesses. There is a knowledge of the Perfection of Reality as the Greater Self gently directs and the lesser self performs in accordance with that direction within its capabilities and the limitations of the conditional world.

In the dimension of temporality, and appearance, Mind experiments with, and in, new form. Sometimes, Mind is gentle, sometimes passive, sometimes placid, sometimes serious, sometimes playful, sometimes violent. **All is Mind** reaching out for new experience. **The Greater Self** suggests and the lesser self acts. Through time the lesser self changes in ability and dimension, its facets coming and going as the creation and investigation of **The Greater Self** requires. All is in perfect order, beauty and harmony. Nothing dies, for **All is One and One Extending, The Universe** in creative play.

SECOND SEASON: As Mind develops memory past rudimentary phase and lodges it in flesh form, memory becomes creature consciousness. In reaching out to do and be more, Mind extending through creature action gives Its lesser self increasing latitude to function and extend more fully. Now, Mind allows Its lesser self to function as though independent of the guidance of **The Greater Self.** Although the guidance is still happening in all events, the lesser self, if it chooses, can blind itself to knowledge of guidance. This allows the lesser self to act as though it is independent and separate.

Guided by Mind, individual consciousness first begins to recognize the shadow and realize that it has the ability to make the shadow move. This becomes reinforced by noticing reflections in water and in certain types of stone. For a long while, the individual human conscious aspect of Mind is fascinated with this phenomenon. It shares this realization with family and others.

Through use of the idea of separation, Mind feels Itself extending, passing barriers that before were limiting the ongoing creation. Mind always dissolves limitation. There is always another way. In finding another way there is a leap of joy, of exultation. This is felt in all aspects of Mind and all respond with encouragement and support.

The lesser consciousness, that aspect of Mind which sees itself as separate and apart, slowly realizes (makes real) form. First it recognizes a difference between itself and other animals and makes difference important.

With the idea of separation from other life forms comes the idea of "death", the horrible thought of changing to some "lesser" form, or, what may seem worse, ceasing to exist. The separate, human aspect of Mind now begins to witness what it sees as the apparent cessation of existence within groups of other creatures like itself and within its own ranks. No longer recognizing union with Mind, it begins to fear the loss of its existence.

THIRD SEASON: Differences begin to dawn rapidly in human consciousness as Mind commits more aspects of Itself to memory within the human intellect. The naming of plants and animals begins, each with its own distinct qualities and its relationship to the human aspect of Mind. The human aspect even names itself, causing further separation from all that it sees as "not human".

Declaring itself superior, it recognizes that it can out perform and out maneuver most other animals and in groups of others, like itself, manage vegetation and animals alike. Sometimes it recognizes its mastery and is proud of "knowing" its separateness and superiority. Sometimes it appreciates mastery and is thankful for knowing it has extended farther than ever before. It is this point in the growth of human consciousness, that humanity begins to recognize and classify differences within itself. All aspects are not alike. Some do not know any separation and act from **Inner Knowledge** of the world's perfection. Some do not allow themselves knowledge of guidance because they do not allow that such guidance is possible. Still others seek to retain the knowledge of Union and guidance knowing their smallness to something they do not understand that is infinitely greater.

There are others also, as Mind produces variety, projecting Itself in every way and yet staying within the abilities of the lesser self. All are the inevitable consequence of Mind complexifying. All play some role in Mind's intention to surpass limits and continue creative extension.

To illustrate the interaction of human consciousness it is necessary to follow the three aforementioned groups through the seasons of human development. For this purpose these groups are divided within the aspect of Extending Mind known as humanity and named. The group not recognizing separation and acting from **Inner Knowledge,** we will call "extenders". The group not acknowledging guidance, "knowing" its separateness and superiority and seeing itself as master we will call "organizers". And the group knowing their smallness and living in awe and respect of that from which it sees itself as separate, we will call "maintainers".

The concept of "death" acts differently on these three aspects of human consciousness. For the extenders, "death" is of no concern. Being and doing is all that is important. Recognizing the need for and inevitability of "death" sets them free to act without restriction. Besides, they would still be what they always were, **The Extending Universe.**

For the organizers, it is important that what one does outlasts the body with which it is done. Through this the separated self hopes to survive. Seeking to be remembered by others for its accomplishments, it achieves what it feels would be remembered. In memory is its continuation assured.

For the maintainers, where human consciousness identifies with the body, only retention of the body is important. Maintaining the body even after it ceases to function with the idea that it will someday function again is their method of surviving and maintaining their differences and separation.

Through naming and expressing and establishing differences, verbal communication begins, first as a combination of gestures and grunts, later as prewords and combinations. Each gesture and sound is weighed by Mind for convenience and effect. Those more effective are retained.

Each aspect of human consciousness has purpose and each performs its function with the talents it is given by Mind as Mind extends through Its aspects in new and creative ways.

FOURTH SEASON: Translation of knowledge begins with the formation of language. Each syllable, each word, each phrase, each sentence is slowly formed in human consciousness as Mind brings awareness of Itself to conscious human attention. A sound cannot be formed without the foundation of air and vibrating substance. A word cannot be formed without a combination of sound. A phrase requires the combination of words; a sentence, the combination of phrases. Every new layer of language construction is placed slowly on the previous foundation. Each element of human language is guided painstakingly by Mind. Each new accomplishment is a cause for rejoicing in The Greater Self.

Now is the season of tribes as each small group extends in its own way, with its own sounds, its own experiences and its own expressions. Some are more verbal, some use more gestures. Some are more expressive in making sounds with wood and sticks or blowing across a blade of grass. The extenders reach out for new means of expression, often borrowing from other tribes. The organizers find expression that fits and is compatible with expression currently used. The maintainers are reluctant to accept anything that is different from the expression they now use.

The extenders express new words and phrases that brings reality into focused attention on a certain aspect of the world of material and circumstance. Organizers, recognizing the value of the expression, verbally compile and memorize these aspects, teaching each word or phrase to maintainers. Maintainers recite verbal differences among themselves, teaching them to each other and to their children.

To the human aspect of mind, this is not without difficulty. For as the extenders suggest new sounds and words into consciousness, there is often a conflict with sounds and words that had already been expressed and seen by the organizers as adequate. Often conflicts arise between the extenders and the maintainers.

The maintainers do not appreciate change and, not seeing themselves as involved in **The Total Process**, they drive extenders from their ranks. Since maintainers comprise the vast majority of a given population, extenders have no choice but to go from tribe to tribe, unless protected by an organizer.

Sometimes maintainers gain power within the tribe and kill or drive out all who seem to be extenders or organizers. This makes the tribe stable but functionally uncreative. Since maintainers do not naturally attract followers, they learn to control through fear of deprivation, torture, or death (by now the idea of death has become a reality for maintainers). Knowing that other maintainer's concern for body is their main motivation, it is easy, with the aid of an extender, to suggest another fear, the fear of the "unknown". With these methods they succeed in keeping tribal order.

It is not long, however, before maintainer led tribes are conquered by a more creative tribe. Usually the leaders of the conquered tribe are put to death or driven out. The children of the tribe are taught the language and customs of the conquering tribe.

When extenders have power, too many new ideas and experiences render the tribe dysfunctional. These tribes are easily conquered by other tribes. For, although they are creative in their own individual way, there is no way they can coordinate their efforts for best results. As a result the tribal society they lead is poorly ordered.

The most functional tribal societies prove to be those where an organizer who recognizes and makes good use of the extenders is in the seat of power. These tribal societies grow in number and flourish as more extenders are drawn to participate in them.

Tribal societies take on more separation from each other and from **The Whole,** with new ideas of ritual, ownership, language and territorial defense. Within the tribe, however, there is little, if any, feeling of individuality or individual ownership. Each member is involved in the greater individual, the tribe.

Through all the apparent human discomfort, Mind

extends the creation, teaching human consciousness, by experience, the most effective methods of hunting, of gathering, of social grouping, of leading. *That which is less effective is guided into a confrontation with that which is more effective.* Either they willingly learn the more effective methods or they are conquered and forced to learn the more effective methods. The only choice is to extend and grow. Every aspect of Mind shows promise in its own way.

Technology begins, first with construction and use of weapons, then control of fire, with counting, with the building of shelter, with use of animals for riding and pulling loads. Each new idea engenders other ideas. The tribal societies that are effective and unafraid of difference grow and prosper.

Here, too, are the beginning traces of religion as those with insight within the tribal society recognize that many problems are caused by social member's inability to act from their inner guidance. "Enablers" (usually extenders) relieve social stress that is the root cause of the problem by aiding the afflicted in reidentifying themselves and their social role. With the social conflict resolved, health returns and both the tribe and the individual benefit. Enablers also train others to follow Mind's Will.

Mind at the separate body level sees itself as gaining life with each new experience, and loosing life as individuals fall in battle, sickness and old age. Mind at the tribal level sees itself as gaining life with each new birth, technical accomplishment or the conquering of another tribe, and losing life when the tribe fails or is conquered by a more effective tribe. Mind at the human level sees itself as gaining more individual beings, more tribes, becoming more effective, expanding, extending, and investigating the far reaches of the earth. **Undifferentiated Mind** experiences only Its continuity and Itself complexifying.

71

FIFTH SEASON: With the growth of human consciousness and population, individuals begin to make differences between one another more important. Most individuals want to be considered special and feel that they are better or greater than one another. This tends to corrupt the creative process and create social conflict within the tribe. Some individuals can recognize this extreme without indulging in it. Others are ignorant of the problems this "thinking" creates and are disruptive.

As extension continues, individual aspects of humanity lose their sense of connectedness. Now they battle among themselves to prove who is the greater, taking one another's belongings, annihilating one another, lying, cheating on agreements, taking advantage of, and physically harming their parents, sexually exploiting whoever is available. Existing in and for themselves, many individual aspects of humanity, seeing themselves completely free and responsible to no one, do whatever gives them momentary pleasure.

Finding themselves completely independent, they trade poisonous food and drink to one another thinking that they alone are doing so. They pleasure themselves with one another's spouses, thinking that it is they alone who do so. They try to enslave one another mentally and physically. Each feels entitled to do whatever enters consciousness, regardless of the effect it has on others. No longer knowing **The One Mind,** an inner part of the individuated consciousness cries for guidance and direction.

As information is translated from the inclusive subconscious to the exclusive conscious mind of humans, they experience themselves as being completely separate and superior to everything that they observe. Since they are given this possibility by Mind as Mind extends, there is no conflict, only a stage that consciousness has to go through to begin to recognize its involvement in **The Greater Self.**

Those who arrive at the greater, more inclusive, understanding more rapidly initiate laws, rules and regulations for their own safety and for the safety of others. This allows for greater freedom of creative enterprise, while those not yet ready to see their involvement are learning what they need to learn. As systems of rule grow, tribes become more and more effective, enlarging and engaging in commerce with other tribes. Soon governments are initiated bringing tribes closer together in common purpose. Monetary systems are initiated allowing trade to happen more easily.

Gatherings for mass training are introduced by organizers. This brings maintainers swiftly into a proficiency in the use of the tribal language, rituals and customs. Those who learn more swiftly are recognized as possible extenders or organizers and tutored by the appropriate tribal elder. Those who show no ability or desire to learn tribal lore are recognized as special and watched for any indication that they may be gifted in some way or troublesome to the tribe at large.

Training is not always pure as some parents try to raise their standing within the tribe by forcing their children to do better than others. When this is recognized by tribal elders, it is discouraged. They know that only those called by their inner guidance to succeed should succeed. In spite of this, though, some members manage to get their children into leadership positions. These children become false extenders and organizers because the **Will of Mind** is not recognized by them.

In and through it all, Mind extends, always enhanced by the learning and accomplishment of its human aspect. Giving direction, It brings together this tribe and that tribe, sometimes in willing compromise and growth, sometimes in battle to determine which is superior. All is within Mind for All is Mind. Every action is a lesson for human consciousness and the learning of that lesson advances the individual, the society and humanity.

Religion is initiated by enablers in every age to express the union between Mind and human consciousness, and to cause individuals to be more in tune with **The Totality of Their Being.** When this happens, the organizers are usually threatened because the enablers have little or no regard for the established system since they see bringing one to an understanding of **The Greater Self** as their only true purpose.

Now and then, false enablers and extenders come into existence and mislead entire populaces. Because of this, organizers do not know who to trust. Believing that their purpose is the establishment of social structure, they see only that someone is trying to institute a new system and rob them of power. Sometimes a religious expression gains too much power and the organizer is unable to excise it from the system. When this happens, organizers find ways to separate the followers from the enabler; then, the religion is turned into a tool to reinforce the existing systems of order and discipline.

The maintainers are seldom aware of what is happening and are perfectly willing, after being persuaded that one language has greater power than another, to follow and recite that which makes their life seem more secure. Organizers, knowing of maintainers mental attachment to the human body aspect of consciousness, the material world, and their fear of and respect for the unknown, distort religion to increase the importance of these attributes. Believing they will somehow avoid "death", the maintainers are easily lead away from true religious expression, into that which is distorted for social purposes.

All existence in the phenomenal world is generated in variety. Mind never allows complexification and individuation without alternate possibilities. Through this, Mind creates balance. On the one hand, Mind can bring more extenders and enablers into power to stimulate and guide creation. On the other hand Mind can give more power to organizers and maintainers with their false extenders and enablers to allow the creation to flow in a way that is unguided. In this manner, Mind, at the level of human consciousness, keeps Its balance on the tightrope of existence.

There is no occurrence in the world of material and circumstance that Mind does not recognize and support. All is managed and actuated by **The Creative, Investigative Force** that is Mind, reaching out for new experience and new expression of Itself in the conditional world. Only the individualized human aspect of Mind would separate that which is convenient from that which is inconvenient and decide that there is someone or something to blame. Mind, not knowing death or suffering, sees the perfection in all that happens.

SIXTH SEASON: As individuals begin to accept social rules and regulations realizing upon the approach of adulthood that rules are mostly for their benefit, so humanity, realizing the need for order if greater creative power is to be acheived, devises governments and enacts laws. First rules are clumsy and oppressive, protecting those who have stolen and declared ownership of the most from those who had stolen the least. These regulations create order while destroying individual initiative.

Mind's attempt to project Its desires into the world of material and circumstance becomes difficult because of the limited amount of knowledge translated from subconscious to human consciousness. With time and more translation, rules become more acceptable and fluent.

By this season, Mind has guided extenders to map the night skies. There is first an awareness of the recurrent appearances and phases of the moon. This becomes an initial guide in knowing when to plant and when to harvest. This is further improved with the naming of constellations and the circumstances that accompany their appearance. Recognizing that certain occurrences are coincidental, the human aspect of consciousness is guided to construct calendars naming time and circumstance of events.

It is also brought to the conscious awareness that there are differences between children born in winter, spring, summer and autumn. Noticing the prevalent constellation becomes a means of predicting human behavior. Sometimes human consciousness feels behavioral differences are due to climatic condition, at other times it sees the cause as being the pattern of the stars.

Mind also guides extenders to initiate alphabets, giving each sound a written symbol. With the initiation of written language, Mind knows that it has broken another limit and in the mind of humanity there is an exhilaration. For a while alphabets pour into the world, each group writing its own based on its own particular sounds. Organizers find that which is compatible and formulate written language. Each state develops its own language but through the influence of extenders who move from state to state, Mind creates similarity and familiarity.

Mind, in translating Itself into human consciousness, always suggests to conscious attention that it is part of and involved in, something greater. The pull of the stars and planets, for a while becomes an abstract means of demonstrating the suggestion, then begins to fall into obscurity as calendars and primitive time measurement devices become available.

Following the direction of organizers, who are not

aware of their continuity with Mind, human consciousness is led to believe that it exists in and for itself with no connection to **The Eternal.** The more it depends on the devices for more effective creation that are suggested by Mind, the less it can know and heed the guidance of Mind. The human consciousness aspect of Mind, thinking itself separate and independent, becomes more and more obsessed with "its own accomplishments" and "its own survival".

Human consciousness, seeing itself as an independently functional creative entity, becomes neglectful of **That Which Causes and Sustains** its thought and action. In denying the existence of that which is greater, it deprives itself of the guidance of that which is greater. In thinking itself small it becomes small and "all else" is "other" and separate. Taking credit for each thought and action, the lesser self praises its ability to create rather than recognizing that it is involved in **The Greater Self, The Extending Universe.** The lesser self becomes enamored by "its creations", not acknowledging that what it did is a product of **All Existence.** By so doing, distortion arises in everything that is produced by the lesser self.

Now is the time humanity finds it necessary to explain its existence. What is distorted most by the lesser self is knowledge of self and its explanation. Explanations about existence take on the character of the explainer, depicting the amount of separation that the explainer experiences. Everything examined is compared to the explainer's estimation of self. Thus animals and plants are higher or lower depending on their approximation to human characteristics. The reality of human consciousness is centered in the decision of what human consciousness considers itself to be. All else is comparative. Till this time, all explanations have been verbal, passed on by maintainers from generation to generation. Now they begin to find their way into the written language.

The product of the lesser self, even its own image, becomes reason for existence. It no longer recognizes or feels the need of The Greater Self. Even in this, it is guided by Mind. The lesser self is free to believe anything it chooses. This does not interfere with Reality. It does, however, allow the lesser self the greatest possible latitude in creative adventure.

The lesser self tends to create reality poorly because of the lack of input from the Greater, more inclusive, Self. This poor creation of reality becomes the cause of illness and social problems in the conditional world. Individuals become more fearful and frustrated, seeing themselves more alone and at odds with the world than they themselves realize (make real).

Enablers, recognizing this problem, try repeatedly to bring the realization of **The Greater Self** to the consciousness of the lesser human self. This meets great resistance from both the organizers and the maintainers. The enabler is usually banished, discredited by organizers, who use terms of their own making in the society that they organize and control, or disrupted by physical annihilation. Annihilation does not solve the problem for the organizers, because anyone who interacts with an enabler has the possibility of becoming a voice for Mind. As a result, annihilation usually increases the protest.

The idea of a XXX* (The symbol used here can be replaced by name of your choice that, for you, is expressive of a supreme deity exclusive of yourself and the world.), separate and distinct from the universe it created, a distortion of the *Knowledge of Mind* becomes useful as a tool of organizers as they seek to perpetuate their own existence and the continuation of the systems that they have instituted.

Many organizers attribute natural occurrences such as floods, earthquakes and cyclones to the wrath of XXX

*see Appendix VI

for maintainer's failure to follow the instructions of organizers. Drawing on the maintainers fear of the unknown, organizers make XXX a symbol for all that they do not know or understand. XXX is always a separate, powerful entity who judges harshly all who fail to follow social guidelines or do not act as those "empowered to know the will of XXX" desire*.

Even this, with all the distortions and erroneous beliefs, becomes useful as Mind extends through the inclination of its human aspect. *All is in order, limits are breached and Mind experiences Itself extending and complexifying as The Creation continues.* Mind does, however, to balance beliefs in separation express through many enablers the idea of Love. This is the realization that nothing is really separate. Enablers, ecstatic with this realization set about persuading the human conscious aspect of Mind of this Truth.

SEVENTH SEASON: Ideas of control and greater systems of control bring forth greater areas of external control. In this season tribes combine through trade or war to become states and then nations. In earlier seasons, rules and regulations are not comprehensive enough to sustain a nation. Now Mind has established natural communal laws in the consciousness of humanity that allow for creation on a large scale through this aspect. Tribal differences are still prevalent, but there is agreement between tribes in matters of commerce and territory.

The more functional tribes are at a place of power, dominating the others. Each nation has its own methods, language and customs. This is guided by Mind as humanity progresses, using the available aspects of human consciousness such as talent and determination. Extenders initiate new methods of bringing people an understanding

*see Appendix VI

of their commonality. Organizers use whatever is compatible and can be recited by the maintainers. Maintainers grumble among themselves but do as they are told.

Each nation establishes identity and sees itself as a separate entity. Extenders, seeing no separation, move freely from nation to nation, just as they moved from tribe to tribe. This establishes a connection between nations. Trade follows. Where nations wall themselves off from each other in fear of losing the identity they have established, war follows. After war, trade follows.

Mind will not be thwarted. Experienced with overcoming natural limitations, the minor limitations imposed by human consciousness are of no consequence. War breaks out. The individual human aspects of humanity which is an aspect of Mind come and go but nothing really changes. The Creation continues. The progress of humanity continues. Human beings come into existence more than replacing those lost in battle. Only human consciousness suffers in its mistaken knowledge of who and what it really is.

Mind brings nations together or keeps them separate as balance and creative interplay require. The Creative Pressure causes each nation to investigate and create free of other influences. When they have developed a wealth of knowledge and become creatively stagnant, they are brought into contact with other nations either through trade or war. Realizations are exchanged and both nations enhanced. This is true, even though, to the separated consciousness of the individual nations, one has won and one has lost.

Extenders, experiencing little or no separation, are not fearful of "loss of life" and treat each new frontier as a challenge. Through them Mind recognizes and dissolves limitation. With each new accomplishment, Mind is enhanced, becoming more complex and more able to meet the next challenge and dissolve the next limitation.

Organizers are more cautious, needing to accomplish something before "loss of life" occurs. Through this they live. Their accomplishment is not always one that benefits humanity. Often it is not. They struggle for power, wealth, fame or infamy. What benefits humanity is a secondary consideration. Through them Mind classifies and regulates the flow of information, bringing together maintainers and causing more active participation in the social process.

Maintainers are most cautious, feeling responsible for their bodies, their group, their religion, their nation, humanity and world conditions. Logged into their memory is the sense of identity and ownership. They are very protective of what they consider themselves to be and to own.

They are told by organizers the way the world "should be" and are encouraged to spend their lives trying to make it be that way. They have no idea what the words of their rituals mean, they only know that these words are important because they are told by their organizer that these are the words of XXX. Through them Mind stabilizes the creation at the level of human consciousness and gives extenders a platform from which to reach outward and upward. Without maintainers, the creation at human level would run amuck and there would be no support for extension.

There are now great battles between nations as Mind extends, deciding on its effectivity at the human level of consciousness. Just as a child may stress the muscle of one arm against the muscle of another to grow and become more powerful, so Mind now brings together parts of Itself lodged in the human aspect to breach limits and extend. Humanity feels this creative pressure and has no choice but to act. The human aspect of Mind does, however, have a choice in the type of action it takes. Even so, it can only act within the limits of its abilities and actualizations.

Great governments come into being which occasionally dominate entire known continents. Like huge waves, one nation grows and swells to maximum prominence; then retreats, only to be replaced by another which rises to an awesome height before breaking on the shore of Eternity. Through it all, Mind searches and probes the world of material and circumstance bringing other aspects of Itself into play for greater creativity.

To the extenders, this is all part of Natural Process and of no real concern. Some throw themselves into the conflict enjoying being involved and knowing that they cannot really be harmed no matter what happens.

Some organizers find this to be advantageous, a chance to become known, a chance to become powerful, a chance to "leave their mark". Others are fearful that they might loose their system, their advantage, their wealth or their power. Still others learn to "roll with the punches" and manage to gain advantage no matter which way the tide of battle turns.

For the maintainers war is very difficult. It concerns the possible loss of possessions, home, family, ideology, life. Everything they believe in is at stake. They must try to keep war in some distant territory away from their homeland. This way, they can enjoy the spoils but not experience the desperation.

Technology, now, has moved from use of stone, natural fibers and hides to use of metals, cement, cloths, fertilizers, natural insecticides, tanned leathers, oil lamps and candles, writing implements and paper. More than ever humanity sees itself as the center of the universe, able to control nature and dominate the animal kingdom.

Mind, through extenders, initiates the translation of

verbal communication into written languages. Through organizers, Mind decides what will be translated and maintainers are given the task of carrying out this directive. The first translations are concerned with social order and law. Second are stories of past actions of humanity. Since the conditional world is a world of beginnings and endings, human consciousness is concerned about its beginnings. All available verbal stories are compared, and the stories that are chosen to be transcribed into writing first are those which organizers feel will have the greatest social benefit.

Mind, through organizers, invites extenders to write stories of heroic exploits. Through this Mind stimulates creation. Extenders, knowing the effect of their words on the groups of their association, create masterful stories about the initiation of humanity, the overcoming of crisis after crisis, the battles of states and nations, and the morality of human kind. Those that organizers find useful are retained, others are discarded or banned from social archives.

Early writing is purposeful. It is not so much to give accurate accounts of happenings within the social group as it is to give the social group members direction in their actions. Each group formulates its own writings and histories. Many times these stories become the main cause of conflict, first between tribes, then between states and later between nations.

Writings, while cementing groups together and stabilizing societies, become a source of conflict as maintainers of one group are frustrated by and tend to fight maintainers of other groups. Not wanting their world to change, they set up obstacles and mental walls to protect themselves from outside influences. This allows them to strengthen their position against other groups "who think and act differently". Each group proclaims its book to be the only "true" book. In creating this difference and making it important they create further separation from each other.

At times, during the translation of Knowledge to the consciousness of the human aspect, human consciousness reaches a state of psychosis. Each group, tribe state or nation considers itself better and more powerful than the others. This is because the group, seeing itself as a separate entity, takes credit for the knowledge that it has translated to consciousness, and feels itself superior to the other, or inferior and must defend itself against the other.

Madness and war ends the separation as the two groups are brought together. The group that is more effective dominates the one that is less effective. They share ideas and concepts. More of their inner knowledge becomes available to their conscious attention. Humanity survives, The Creation continues and Mind dissolves another barrier in Its progress toward bringing Itself to the attention of human consciousness.

Thus it is that all barriers devised by organizers and supported by maintainers are doomed to failure. **That Which Is Not Separate** knows no limits, only temporary impediments to Its ongoing flow, breaches all barriers, blending the impounded elements into greater being. That which is aware never suffers during this process. Only that which is ignorant and strives to maintain its difference suffers.

EIGHTH SEASON: Strife continues within the aspect of human consciousness known as humanity. War, disease, famine and pestilence pervade the world of material and circumstance as Mind brings new realizations to the attention of human consciousness. Each obstacle to be conquered by humanity brings human consciousness closer to a realization of its true nature.

Where the separated self takes credit or blame, it fails the lesson and must relearn. Where it sees itself as part of and involved in **The Continuing Creative Process,** it gains the knowledge and awareness necessary to overcome these obstacles.

Now, there is a profusion of creation as Mind acting more and more through Its human aspect brings industry into existence. Human abilities surpass the understanding of human consciousness. Human explanations credit individual human aspects of Mind with breakthroughs and accomplishment, erecting monuments to them in an effort to spur on more creation.

In poor understanding of Total Process one nation vies against another. Competition, between individuals, between groups and religions, between states, and between nations, becomes the practice of this season. Continual strife and conflict become a way of life.

Human consciousness, not recognizing yet that it is Mind extending, takes credit for all "its" accomplishments. In creating devices and chemicals of destruction it declares itself separate and superior to all other creatures, annihilating those it feels serve "no useful purpose", or are considered harmful to "human progress".

Mind, defining Itself as a certain nation hides its accomplishments and realizations from other nations in order to gain and retain superiority. Thus, Mind, in Its ongoing flow creates obstacles that greatly enhance The Creation for the moment but must be overcome as The Creation continues.

Mind, defining Itself as a group or religion, sees only the difference it has declared important and the superiority of its beliefs. Guarding against the influence of other systems and beliefs it creates obstacles to overcome.

Mind, defining Itself as an individual, sees only the difference between itself and other individuals. Holding secret its inner thoughts and reasoning, it portrays what it more often, sees as functional in the world of material and circumstance. Sometimes, it does so in fun and laughter but, more often it does so in competition and anger. Guarding itself against the danger of being taken over or loss of its individuality, it creates obstacles to be overcome.

In the translation of Mind into human consciousness, this is the season of total immersion in the external, conditional world. Extenders are ignored except for ideas that make one nation, one group or one individual seem "better" than another. These are the only suggestions that seem practical or useful to the twisted consciousness of human conflict. This is a season of madness where Mind acting through one group, attempts to annihilate Mind acting through another.

Religion founded to be the *bearer of Truth and the wisdom of recognizing one's involvement in* **The One Mind***, is subtly redirected by organizers to reflect their own sense of insecurity and personal ambitions. Members are convinced that if they do and say the right thing in the right way they will be spared suffering, grief, and physical and economic illness. They believe that they will be more prosperous than those who think and act in some other way.

Many understand that if they do and act "just right" they will be able to avoid "death" or be brought back from "the dead". While there is an element of truth in what is being expressed and what is being witnessed, most organizers, not knowing **The Truth of Their Existence** cannot share It or lead others to It. The aspect of Mind which is human consciousness is invited, by the unaware, to fix on that which is superficial and irrelevant to greatness. In

*see Appendix VI

86

doing so, it fails to recognize that which is Real.

Each group calls upon XXX to protect it and give it victory over the other. Each sees itself as the only group in touch with XXX. All other groups are faulty and must be subdued. The human aspect of Mind, separated further by religious differences, calls upon XXX to intercede for it against other parts of Itself. Often, in doing so, it feels that it has gained the necessary power and throws itself into combat with the other aspect of Self.

It is in this season that Mind experiences maximum creative flow through the conflicts of human consciousness. Of all the seasons of human development, this is the most critical. The decisions made here either allow the translation to be completed, destroy that possibility for this aspect of Mind, or cause the human consciousness aspect of Mind to muddle about in the eighth season, never capable of self fulfillment or self destruction.

The eighth season is the natural outgrowth of thought systems initiated in the fifth and sixth seasons. Humanity has taken a certain passage in the maze of understanding and must investigate it to the place where investigation can go no farther. This is a time of maximum advance in all aspects of human consciousness.

Extenders are prominent, testing every avenue of possibility. They express new concepts and discoveries and their concern for their unwise use. Schools begun in the sixth and seventh seasons are now modified to create more extenders as each nation strives to outdo the other. False extenders are created with the ability to extend within a given discipline but they have little overview and a great sense of separation.

False extenders are increasingly used in mass educational systems as enablers. Each generation becomes more and more separate from The Reality of Mind as false enablers beget more false enablers and extenders. Instead of being in tune with **The Reality of Mind,** organizers and maintainers rely on the reality of the system they have created and hold dear.

Organizers use the new discoveries to protect their systems paying little attention to the concerns of real extenders. Relying more and more on false extenders they build weapons of war and destruction. Each nation seeks to demonstrate its superiority over the other. The weapons are used heedless of the direction of the extenders who know **The Greater Will** and speak for Mind.

Maintainers, following the direction of their organizer, band together to protect themselves from the enemy that their organizer has declared. They know that they must win or die. Each group performs its rituals, and recites its creed and beliefs and sees the "threat" of other creeds and beliefs.

Major wars break out. Devices of massive destruction are released destroying entire populations. Each new device inspires a new device as organizers disregard the advice of the true extenders and enablers. Using false extenders, nations, led by misguided organizers and urged by their panicked maintainers, attempt to destroy each other out of a false belief in their own mastery or out of fear.

Mind experiences great achievement as complexification is maximized, but realizes the Self-limiting nature of allowing Its human aspect total freedom of choice. Toward the end of this season Mind, through the aspect of human consciousness, reaches a limit in creative expression through violence.

There is a growing clarity that continued construction of weapons and waging of war is not only a sterile pursuit but also detrimental to that aspect of Mind known as humanity. Because of the complexity and sophistication of weaponry, another major conflict would seriously inhibit Mind's ability to complexify through humanity.

Now is a time similar to the fifth season before rules and laws came into effect. There is a general creative paralysis as individuated aspects of human consciousness recognize the blatant faults of competitive enterprise. Each group tries to capture the market with cheaper prices and shoddier goods. They have no concern about placing chemicals in the marketplace that will poison others, destroy the atmosphere or the land.

Organizers, assured by false extenders and enablers from a corrupted educational system, do whatever they can to gain the most money, prominence and power. Seeing themselves as separate entities, not involved in **The Ongoing Creation,** they cheat one another, steal from one another, cheat their members and maintainers, and pollute the vital fluids and firm materials of planets rendering them uninhabitable.

False religions pray to XXX to give them money and power to overtake and overturn other false religions.

Within the consciousness of humanity, there is a growing dissatisfaction of the quality of their leadership. Individuals refuse to participate in warfare. Students revolt against false enablers within the educational system. Many students, seeing the falseness of the system, leave to learn on their own. There is a great unrest as human consciousness, knowing the futility of further extension through warfare, feels the pressure to act, but experiences poor guidance as to the direction that action is to take place.

Everywhere, there is a consciousness of the futility of continued growth through conflict. Maintainers leave their respective groups and join in subcultures where love or fear is the primary expression. Many experiment with substances that will alter their *mental arrangement.* Many leave the world of material and circumstance because they cannot reconcile the world of conflict and **The World of Love.**

Some organizers see their world falling apart and try desperately to shore up their organizations against the onslaught of the awesome power that is being released through the expressions of Truth and Love. Since they live in the separation that they have made real, they are in total and irreconcilable fright of what will happen to themselves, their organizations and to the world if *Truth, the realization that there is but one purpose and everything that exists is involved in that purpose,* and *Love, the realization that nothing is really separate,* gain a foothold.

Since their power is derived from declaring and maintaining a separation between their organization along with other, perhaps similar but not quite as good, organizations, and all organizations that do not recognize and recite the "proper" expressions, they cannot possibly condone expressions of Truth or Love. Sometimes they pretend, but they know where to draw the line.

Other organizers, and would be organizers, see this as an opportunity. Recognizing the weakness in their leader's expressions and policies they start new organizations taking as many members with them as possible. False religions spring up in abundance. Some harken back to early reliance on stars and planets to predict natural occurrences before calendars accurately fixing time became a more convenient instrument. Many use maintainer's fear of and respect for the unknown to gain followers. Some organizers give themselves credentials by purporting to be the voice of some ancient and wise person.

For the most part organizers of these false religions enable themselves while disabling others. Realizing separateness, they seek to organize that which they see as separate. Realizing superiority, they seek to train that which they see as inferior. Realizing fear, they seek to change or contain that which they see as threatening. Realizing their perfection, they seek to modify that which they see as imperfect. Realizing exclusivity, they deny inclusivity. Realizing smallness, they deny greatness.

Often the aspect of mind that is herein known as human consciousness does not finish the eighth season of human development. In realizing smallness and separation in and through all its subsequent aspects, the human consciousness aspect of Mind destroys itself in pollution, power grabbing and fear rather than recognizing its union with Mind, Truth and Love.

Now is a time when all types of religious expression are trotted before **The Eye of Mind** for review. Mind, knowing none to be better or worse, speaks more fluently through those which can better hear and better express Truth and Love. Through the others Mind speaks as their systems of division and separation allow.

NINTH SEASON: The unrest continues in human consciousness as Mind searches for new directions of unfoldment. In humanity this demonstrates as the use of chemical devices to reach deeper, more expanded levels of consciousness. Many disable themselves in their effort. Maintainers who achieve some realizations of greater being develop followings and become organizers. Organizers who manage through ingestion of chemicals or practice of meditation to become more aware, recognize how petty their concerns were and become enablers.

Mind, now through every means available, brings Itself to conscious human attention. Extenders and enablers are multiplied to offset the false extenders and enablers engendered by social educational systems and personal interest groups. For individual searchers this begins with a rare insight. The searcher either follows this thread and is enhanced in thoughts, words and actions, or ignores it to keep the familiar world intact.

Decisions made in the eighth season begin to take effect. Human consciousness that does not make the right decisions in the eighth season does not come into the ninth season either because they are not willing to let go of the decisions that hold them back or because those societies did not survive the eighth season.

Human consciousness having arrived at the ninth season has set aside individual and group hostility. Knowing the problems caused by creating arbitrary divisions, declaring them real and then choosing to defend them in battle, human consciousness now relaxes. Now it knows that the best way to do anything is to allow decisions to be in the "hands of a higher power". It demonstrates time and again that when each of the disputing parties give up that which they consider best for themselves, a "higher power" decides what is best for all concerned. Both parties know the truth of it and the dispute ends with both parties gaining wisdom and knowledge.

Realizing that there is not a great separation between humanity and other creatures, groups form to enable and protect from needless suffering or extinction all creatures, large and small, aware or dumb, attractive or repulsive.

The aspect of Mind known as human consciousness begins to realize that it is not separate from the air that the body breathes, the fluids that it drinks or the food that it eats. Through this awareness, it recognizes its commonality with all creatures and with the environmental system wherein it resides.

As Mind reaches out for greater contact with its human aspect, so now the consciousness of humanity turns from its dream of separation and superiority to the realization of its union with **Mind and with All of Creation.**

TENTH SEASON: Those following the thread of Truth grow and diversify, each knowing involvement in **The Ongoing Creation.** Each expresses the talents they have as an aspect of Mind. Not wanting more nor settling for less, they demonstrate the joy of knowing their union with each other and **The Union of The Universe.**

The element of human consciousness that has not yet awakened to its **Real Self** or its **Limitless Possibilities** can only stand in wonder and awe of what it witnesses, still fearful of letting go of its smallness. Unable to reconcile the "unknown" and its smallness, it tries desperately to cling to its smallness which it feels that it knows.

In time the lesser consciousness disappears as it is swallowed up in **The Greater Self.** Now humanity operates in concert, sharing each new development in excited wonder as it is experienced. Now, in the body of humanity as in **The Body of Mind** each movement enhances all other movements. Each moment is a lifetime as each new experience reverberates in Mind and is amplified ten-thousand-fold within the human consciousness.

Whenever there is any possible conflict, now, within the body humanity, Mind knows and Mind tells all. Humanity knowingly adjusts because the experience of its involvement in Mind is the only thing that is real. Unwilling to trade this experience for less, every individuated self and every individualized cell within the body humanity as within the body life accept the guidance of Mind, knowing Its perfection in all things.

With no one to fight and nothing withheld, Mind, and the aspect of Mind known as humanity, know Union and the struggle through seasons of translation is only a dream, a memory somewhere in the recesses of consciousness that need never be reviewed again.

Realizations:

You and I may be living in different seasons of human development. It is important to understand that no season is better than another. Sometimes our mental arrangement slips back into earlier seasons. Sometimes it projects forward into seasons we are yet to experience in the conditional world. The season in which any person or group of people dwells is the place for them to be. Thus they experience what they need to experience in order to perfect their mental arrangement.

Anytime the aspect of Mind referred to herein as humanity believes that there is something other than Mind, it slips back into earlier seasons and must work its way forward again.

Individuals slip back into the fifth and sixth seasons from time to time, but, now, there are enough in the ninth and tenth season who can remind them of who and what they really are and pull them forward.

Even in the ninth and early tenth season there are still battles and scrimmages waged by those who dwell in earlier seasons, but they are not severe and are quickly settled.

In later seasons, there are many extenders and enablers. Organizers function mainly to promote extenders and their works, knowing that this is their contribution to the system and through it they live. Maintainers, now, have at least a decent philosophy; one that enables them rather than enslaves them.

Chapter VII

THE POWER OF DECISION*

All ideas and acts in *the world of material and circumstance* are the result of decision. Without decision, no thing exists and nothing happens. It is by decision and decision alone that the world is released from sameness and continuity and transformed into the multifaceted creation that human consciousness witnesses and calls reality.

The initiating decision, which is always constant, is that *The Creation shall continue.* All other decisions are subsequent to this decision. Every time a decision is made, no matter how small or insignificant it may appear, it is the result of the primordial decision that creation shall happen. Since this is so, all acts and occurrences experienced in the world of material and circumstance are the result of **The Ongoing Creation.**

No course of action affects the initial decision nor can this decision be changed or altered in any way. Any subsequent decision is either creative or investigatory in nature, even a decision to ignore the initial decision and pretend not to be affected by it.

To decide that there is no Ongoing Creation or that The Creation is something that happened long ago and is no longer relevant to life is to decide in conflict with **The Primary and All Inclusive Decision** and the experiences of life. Since this decision cannot be real, as is evidenced by the writing and reading of this passage, the millions of vital acts that continually enhance the quality of life, the gradual development of the way each aspect of consciousness views and experiences life, and the changes observed from day to day, the decision that there is no Ongoing Creation can only be pretended.

* see Appendices VIII and IX

Deciding that there is no Ongoing Creation leaves consciousness powerless in the world of material and circumstance. When this happens, consciousness must react blindly to circumstances from which it considers itself as separate and, therefore, beyond its control.

The realization that The Creation is continuous and ongoing is sufficient to open the doors of awareness. This is the first decision that consciousness must make in order to approach Reality. Without this decision, consciousness remains separated, fearful, conflicted and blind to its own operation. With this realization, consciousness reflects on its own operation, recognizing its power and possibility.

Subsequent decisions are made as the growth of conscious reality happens. Each decision brings into focus a new experience. Each new experience produces a new realization and each new realization enhances the existing reality. As reality grows, previous realizations that become fixed and familiar are no longer interesting. This is the platform from which consciousness reaches, making decisions and gaining new experience.

Each decision not in conflict with previous decisions empowers consciousness, allowing for growth and accomplishment that is not conflicted. Aspects of consciousness that operate from a reality in which there is no conflicting decisions experience harmony, power, peace and joy as consciousness makes new decisions and harvests new experience.

When a decision is made that is in conflict with decisions already fixed in reality, there is a dissonance. This must be resolved or the aspect is robbed of power and subsequent decisions are in conflict and disorder. Illness and disease are the result of failure to resolve conflicting decisions. When dissonance is resolved, symptoms disappear.

Every decision has within it **The Power of Mind**. When there is a conflict with an earlier decision, this Power is reduced by a factor that is proportional to the amount of conflict. The resulting experience has an equivalent distortion and departs from **The Truth of Being** by the degree which conflict determines. All subsequent decisions and experiences are effected by this deviation and stray farther, substantially diminishing the effective power available to the deciding aspect of consciousness.

Effective creation depends on the amount of power available to an aspect of consciousness. With each conflicting decision, the available power is diminished significantly. Alternately, with every resolution of conflict this power is increased significantly. As conflict is resolved, an aspect approaches union with Mind and union of Mind, gaining the power that was lost through conflicting decisions.

In the world of material and circumstance, it is necessary to direct the use of power so that there is no conflict between participating aspects. Mind directs Its aspects to operate in such a way that there is minimum conflict and maximum effective creation. As the aspects recognize their involvement in **The Ongoing Creation**, effective creation is maximized and they are rewarded with greater power.

Aspects of consciousness always have the possibility of misusing power by deciding to operate in a conflicted manner. This renders them creatively ineffective, as Mind uses other aspects of consciousness to balance their operation. As each individualized aspect becomes aware of its misuse of power through recognizing its involvement in **The Greater Self,** it not only frees itself for more effective creation but also frees its balancing aspect.

Aspects that create ineffectively due to conflicted decisions endeavor to gain power from aspects that are more effectively creative. Inviting the more effective aspects to give them power, they lead the effective aspects toward ineffectivity. Every time they gain power through misleading another aspect they experience a reward and justification for their actions.

Because these aspects of creation see themselves as separate and not involved in **Mind** or **The Ongoing Creation**, they develop exclusive relationships and require opposition to maintain their power. The result is conflict and ineffective creation. The power they have managed to gain in this manner is sooner or later dissipated, and their potential, along with the potential of misled aspects, and the potential of the aspects used as counterbalance, is wasted as a creative force.

In and through all action, Mind, undifferentiated, and, therefore, unaware of, or concerned about, the particulars, empowers its varied aspects to act in accordance with the decisions they have made. Since all decisions made in consciousness are decisions made by Mind, they receive the power that is required to carry them to fruition. When that power brings aspects into conflict, the resulting dissonance is decided by "annihilation" of the lesser aspects, subjugation of the lesser aspect to the greater aspect, or by resolution that results in the cooperation of the lesser and greater aspects. Whatever the outcome, Mind is enhanced.

At lesser levels of consciousness where conflict seems real, Mind acts through Its aspects in such a way that there is a maximum flow of creative power. Often, aspects, acting at lower levels of consciousness, experience an enhancement of their power when involved in conflict. This is reason enough for them to cause and sustain conflict. To resolve the conflict that empowers them deprives them of their power. Only when they experience power in some other manner, are they capable of releasing conflict as a means of causing power experiences.

Often, the organizing aspect of consciousness invites the maintainer aspect to remain blind to **The Ongoing Creation**. This keeps organization more in control causing maintenance to come to it for answers. Maintenance believes what it is told to believe and does not question because it is told not to question. Thus organization may look farther and experience more viewpoints but not accept that maintenance can understand.

To maintainers, organizers are knowledgeable and authoritative. To organizers, maintainers seek only the bliss of ignorance, the pleasure of frivolity, security to a ripe old age and an assured hereafter where all is perfect and nothing harmful or unpredictable will happen. It is here that much of the power of maintainers is invested. In providing services that support the desires and decisions of maintainers, organizers keep maintainers dependent and in their control. Organizers also provide the required distraction that helps maintainers avoid recognizing their talents and purpose.

While maintainers invest most of their power in the superficial comforts in the world of material and circumstance, organizers invest their power in doing that which is memorable and respectable. Here, they endow the world of material and circumstance with the ability to judge them on their performance and reward them with fame and fortune.

When this happens they attain social power, when it does not, they are frustrated and despondent. Their fulfillment lies in the recognition and appreciation received from others through their efforts to modify, or make stable, the world of material and circumstance.

Extenders are continually changing the way they view

the world of material and circumstance, and, therefore, the way it appears to them. Keeping before them the realization that there is no certain way the conditional world is, they try different ways of seeing in order to become more creatively expressive. Recognizing the psuedo-stability that is the invention of organizers, they avoid it to pursue other interests and release their talents without barriers.

Living with the realization that there is only **The Ongoing Creation** in which they (and everything else) is involved, they operate only from their inner guidance or the truth of their being. Here, they find direction and a real sense of stability when they do as they are called in **The Ongoing Creation**. Since all external rewards have limited appeal and are usually an invention of organization to cause and maintain conformity, they seek only the internal rewards of knowing they did what they were called to do and the accompanying *sweep of awareness* that brings them to new understanding. To extenders, power has nothing to do with controlling others or stabilizing the world. Being powerful is having the ability to see from the maximum number of different viewpoints, and experiencing involvement in **The Ongoing Creation**.

Extenders who are enablers decide to use their talents to bring about a *portal of perception* in the *mental arrangement* of others. Not realizing a separation from others, they cause in others what they would cause in themselves, *the sweep of awareness*. In causing the sweep, and recognizing how they caused the sweep, they are rewarded with new insight and awareness themselves. To them, power is a meaningless concept used only by those less knowledgeable.

Those in whom they cause the *sweep of awareness* are renewed and begin to operate from a different *mental arrangement*. When a new *mental arrangement* in any aspect of consciousness is inclusive of its cause, it broadens, becoming greater than it was before the sweep of awareness. When it is exclusive of its cause, it narrows becoming less that it was before the sweep.

Through all activity in the world of material and circumstances, it is the process of deciding which either enhances or depletes effective creative power. Each decision is made by Mind through one of Its aspects. If the decision is in conflict with previous decisions, or the decisions of other aspects, it is because of distortions introduced into the decision making process at lesser (more exclusive) levels of consciousness.

Aspects of consciousness that operate as though they were exclusive and independent, develop conflicted mental arrangements and experience the consequence of their decisions. When they feel that the results are beneficial, they continue along the decision path that they have chosen. When they find the results detrimental, they change their decision path, usually selecting a path that is in direct opposition.

When aspects of human consciousness find that they are unable to function effectively because their decisions are in conflict with other decisions they have made, or in conflict with the decisions made by "others", they either continue their pattern and remain ineffective, or they give others the power and responsibility of deciding for them. When they give up the power of decision, they relegate themselves to a maintainer *mental arrangement.* At the same time, though, they rise to a new, more inclusive, level of consciousness.

Here, they are recognizing something more inclusive that they must depend upon if they are to achieve effective creation. Giving their power to an organizer, they declare themselves inadequate to make decisions that are not detrimental to their own wellbeing.

The organizer aspect of consciousness is ready and willing to receive this power and, in fact, solicits it through its activities and the activities of its maintainers. In getting together followers to produce creative works, it demonstrates its power and invites more of those operating from conflicted decisions into its "fold". With every new maintainer enlisted, the power of the decision making organizer is increased. This happens independent of the particular belief system promulgated by the organizing aspect.

In an effective system, the organizing aspect uses power that has been granted to it by the maintainer aspect, to enhance creation, by making decisions that empower the maintainers. In an ineffective system, the organizing aspect takes credit for the accomplishments of the system and keeps the maintainers from the experience of their own power.

In the giving and receiving of power*, there is a delicate balance. Decisions made at different levels of consciousness must dovetail in such a way that maximum creative power is released and the individuals involved experience fulfillment. When this does not happen, there is a source for conflict that only the restructuring of invested power can resolve.

Realizations:

You and I are involved in The Ongoing Creation. It is through our thoughts and actions that the creation extends. When we make decisions that are in harmony with The Ongoing Creation, our power is enhanced. When we make decisions that are in conflict with The Ongoing Creation, or with our previous decisions, our power is decreased.

If you or I are having difficulty, it is because we have forgotten our basic decision, have decided a reality that is

* see Appendix VIII

in conflict with the primary decision, and are holding the wrong things important. Or, maybe, we are just trying to make a decision that is in conflict with some earlier decision.

We rob ourselves of power with each conflicting decision that we make. This results in frustration, fear and illness. As we resolve the conflicts the symptoms disappear.

If you feel powerless, it is because you have invested your power in some person, idea or circumstance and endowed it with the ability to control you. If you had invested it wisely, your power would be multiplied and you would feel powerful and fulfilled.

There are certain powers that you have given up. When you find them again, all will be in perfection for your world will unfold beautifully and bountifully.

You and I give power to others. Accordingly, we operate at the level we have chosen to invest our power. When we give our power to conflict, either by causing it or trying to prevent it, the idea of conflict is our reality.

No one ever gets to a greater level of consciousness unless they are able to let go of their ineffective mental arrangement. When they do let go, they must build a mental arrangement with more power because they have taken their power away from where it was invested.

That which you or I do not create by giving it our power does not exist. When we succumb to the idea that we are victims, we create a circumstance in such a way that it robs us of our power. When we decide that the circumstance we have encountered is a challenge to be overcome, we surprise ourselves with the power we have to overcome it.

A Person of Knowledge knows that to which power is given and that from which power is derived. Knowing that power used in and derived from conflict, except when this power is used to resolve the conflict, is power ill used, a Person of Knowledge uses power only for creativity that is unconflicted and the creative resolution of conflict.

Chapter VIII

FACTORS OF CREATION

THE CREATION OF REALITY

True Reality is unreasonable. Having no limits or divisions It defies expression. Being timeless, It defies explanation. Being dimensionless, It defies measure. That which is expressed in the world of material and circumstance is always less than Reality. What is measured is the result of a decision to differentiate.

That which is known to the human aspect of consciousness as reality is the result of systematically dividing **That Which Is Whole and Indivisible.** The human aspect sees this, however, as adding more knowledge. Every time it names an aspect of Reality, it pretends that the aspect so named is separate and distinct from all other aspects.

Reality does not come to the consciousness of humanity suddenly, in one giant leap of understanding, but slowly, in bits and pieces. Sounds are recognized before letters, letters, before words, and words, before sentences. Knowledge is a procession of symbols displayed before the eye of the human mind depicting an aspect of **The Greater Undifferentiated Self.**

As human consciousness reaches out for new understanding and new expression, reality grows. There is no place where it is complete and whole, only places where it has become inclusive of the expressions and experiences it has encountered. That which consciousness has set in place is taken for granted and neglected. It is only in encountering different expressions and having new experiences that consciousness has the opportunity to recognize its incompletion and expand to become "more whole".

All opportunity for expansion is at the periphery of

the familiar understanding that human consciousness maintains and holds to be real. It is not until consciousness relaxes its hold on what it deems to be real that it can become inclusive of these peripheral expressions and extend in their direction. Till then, consciousness must see other expressions as foreign and ignore them.

All aspects of consciousness develop reality through the same progression. It is the same for the individual as it is for the for the family, for the organization, for the nation and for humanity. Reality, in the world of material and circumstance, is a product of time and a consequence of experience.

MENTAL ARRANGEMENT

What human consciousness holds to be real is only circumstantial. It is an arrangement of the bits and pieces of Reality (which is indivisible), within the aspect of human consciousness, that is seen by human consciousness as real. This *mental arrangement* is a product of experience and impression in the conditional world. *Every aspect of consciousness experiences the conditional world differently and, therefore, develops a different mental arrangement.*

Since no two *mental arrangements* are exactly alike, each being born of different realizations, reality cannot be the same. The creation of reality, through the arrangement of mental impressions, is subject to the whim of the creator at the level of operation decided within the *canyon of conceit.*

Within the *mental arrangement* are all classifications and decisions, tagged by the classifier with the appropriate amount of importance, in accordance with the reality already decided. These familiar classifications and decisions are kept before consciousness and used as a "yardstick" with which to measure new information and experiences.

Growth or reality expansion is not so much a matter of memorizing new information as it is of changing the *mental arrangement* with which expressions and experiences are being measured. When this happens, clarity is achieved and that which was not acceptable to the more restrictive *mental arrangement* becomes obvious in the more inclusive arrangement.

THE ADVENTURE QUOTIENT
Within a given *mental arrangement* and based on prevalent circumstances at the onset of that arrangement, there is a need for freshness or newness. This need is experienced by the aspect of consciousness as a type of pressure demanding action in a new and unusual way. It is especially felt when experiences in the conditional world become too familiar and redundant. The human aspect of Mind then knows that it has thoroughly digested all the information available and is now ready to receive more. It is at this point that there is a heightened interest in the happenings in the world of material and circumstance. It is then, too, that the *mental arrangement* has become modified and prepared for acceptance of new expression.

Alternately, when the consciousness of the human aspect is full of information and experiences that have not been classified or included in the *mental arrangement*, there is a pressure to avoid newness or strangeness. This avoidance continues until such time as a shift in the way reality is mentally arranged occurs. While avoidance is happening, new or unfamiliar expression is not acceptable and, often, not even tolerable.

The amount of needed or acceptable adventure varies with an aspects ability to change its *mental arrangement*. Therefore, reality growth is dependent on this factor. Since most aspects of human consciousness are of a maintainer nature, it is extremely difficult to bring about reality growth without regeneration. Since they maintain the *mental arrangement* produced by circumstances of early environment, change can only happen through rec-reation of early environment situations.

As human consciousness realizes that its reality is ap-pended to circumstance that has been encountered, it learns to create new circumstance that will modify its at-tachment to the previous circumstance. In doing so, it real-izes that it is in control of its reaction to circumstance and, therefore, in control of its own *mental arrangement.* As human consciousness learns to modify its own *mental ar-rangement,* it finds itself called to more and greater adven-ture.

THE DEFENSE-CONTROL MECHANISM

The *defense-control mechanism* is an integral part of any *mental arrangement.* This allows the aspect conscious-ness to process information with minimal interference from external sources. Having established a reality, the aspect must retain it until such time as it becomes ineffec-tive by weight of evidence. (The maintainer's evidence de-pends primarily on the decision of its organizer.)

This mechanism is in effect whenever expression is too far from the periphery of the aspect's reality and the gap in understanding cannot be bridged without totally abandoning the familiar *mental arrangement,* the imping-ing expression is already included and redundant, or the aspect is processing as much material as can be handled at this time without loss of continuity.

THE CIRCLE OF CERTAINTY

With the *defense-control mechanism* an aspect of human consciousness endeavors to fend off expression and experience that may cause a change in *mental arrangement.* If the aspect is successful it experiences a "circle of certainty". No longer spiraling outward and experiencing change, it begins operating from a fixed reality.

In doing so, the aspect of consciousness decides that it knows how the world is and will defend its reality against all challenges from other aspects. It will also attempt to persuade other aspects of the "truth" of its reality so that comfort can be assured.

While an aspect of consciousness is concentrating on maintaining a circle of certainty, no growth of reality is possible. Here, the decision has been made to exclude, at least for this time, all factors that may cause a change in the existing *mental arrangement.* (Circles of certainty are common for aspects of Mind operating at the maintainer level, frequent for aspects which are organizational and unusual for aspects which are extenders or enablers.)

THE PORTAL OF PERCEPTION
The development of human consciousness takes place in the world of material and circumstance. There are only certain times and circumstances during which new growth may take place. Anything offered or experienced during these times can become part of an aspect's reality, permanently changing its *mental arrangement.*

This *portal of perception* is brought about by a relaxation, or a realization of the ineffectivity, of the *defense-control mechanism* which an aspect of consciousness finds operationally valid. This is seen by human consciousness as a "time of Divine revelation", "religious experience", etc. This is a time when the consciousness of the aspect reviews its *mental arrangement.* In this moment division does not exist. There is only the ability to decide on possible divisions and the amount of importance to be afforded each.

It is in this moment that the decision is made to arrange reality in a manner that is inclusive or exclusive of that which is impinging on the periphery of the familiar *mental arrangement*. This is the space where true change is possible and **True Reality** is approachable.

All subsequent occurrences in the conditional world are the result of decisions made in this moment. Where exclusion is decided, the resulting *mental arrangement* approaches ignorance and conflict. Where inclusion is decided, the resulting *mental arrangement* approaches harmony and wisdom.

THE SWEEP OF AWARENESS

Decisions made in the *portal of perception* always result in a *sweep of awareness* due to review of the *mental arrangement* within control of a certain aspect. There is always some shift in *mental arrangement* and, therefore, always a period of adjustment. This period of adjustment, and its subsequent acceptance of new expression, is determined by the length and strength of the pre-existing *mental arrangement* in comparison to a new possiblity.

The *sweep of awareness* is inclusive of the opening of the portal of perception which initiated the review, the review itself, the comparison of alternative possibilities, and the enhanced learning condition following the decision to include or exclude that which opened the portal.

When a decision to exclude is made, the *sweep of awareness* continues until the necessary information is logged into the *defense-control mechanism* of the *mental arrangement*. This includes a retention in memory of what initiated the portal of perception, a blockage of the memory of details of the expression or experience to be excluded, and a subsequent reclassifying of similar expressions or experiences to be avoided. When the aspect of consciousness is satisfied that it has protected itself from further threat to the familiar reality, the *sweep of awareness* subsides and the aspect resumes familiar patterns of operation within a *circle of certainty* at greatly reduced intensity.

When a decision to include is made, the *sweep of awareness* continues until the *mental arrangement* of the aspect of consciousness adjusts to include the new circumstance, expression or experience. This includes the details of the expression or experience gauged from various viewpoints, comparison of other similar possibilities, an investigation of all experience and expression at the periphery of the familiar reality, a subsequent modification of the existing *mental arrangement* for maximum inclusion, and the exploration of ideas and material that might be relevant in the new reality.

When the aspect of consciousness is satisfied that it has learned all it can from the circumstance or expression that opened the *portal of perception* and initiated the evaluation of reality, it begins to operate from the new reality in an enhanced state of awareness. All subsequent learning is greatly accelerated until the body of relative material and ideas is exhausted or the *mental arrangement* proves to be inadequate for further reception. Then consciousness returns to a reduced speed of operation within the *circle of certainty* of its now familiar reality.

THE POWER SPIRAL

At the onset, consciousness does not know limits or boundaries. In the human aspect of Mind it performs the function of inquirer into the world of material and circumstance. There are no recorded differences of remembered experiences. There is only a reaching outward into an unexplored world.

As differences become apparent and are remembered, consciousness enters into the world of contrasts. At this time there is a cataloging of differences but no label of importance is yet attached. The primary concern of consciousness at this time is in getting acquainted with the material aspect of Reality, recognizing and using primary abilities within the material aspect, and maintaining the faculties that cause and allow this extension.

Now is the beginning of *the power spiral*. As the aspect's reality is being constructed with bits and pieces of contrast in the world of material and circumstance, the aspect of consciousness becomes more active, exploring the possibilities of further extension. At this time, the *sweep of awareness* is extensive as consciousness of the aspect which is now becoming definite and material rushes from one new realization to another.

At times, this onward rush is slowed by circumstances remembered in a disconcerting way, causing the spiral to become circular. At these times, extension ceases as consciousness stays with a now familiar reality and operates within the confines of its *circle of certainty.*

Occurrences in the conditional world tend to break the *circle of certainty* causing a new *portal of perception* and the consequential *sweep of awareness.* The aspect of consciousness is then thrown out tangentially from the circle and, unless inhibited by a decision of exclusion in the defense-control mechanism, begins spiraling outward to new realizations and a new, more inclusive, sense of reality.

This process continues within the conscious realm through all aspects of consciousness. Each individualized aspect acts within the framework that is available to it in the world of material and circumstance. The more unique, different, special, separate and exclusive it defines itself to be, the more it must protect the borders of its reality against the incursion of what it has decided that it is separate from and better than.

CAUSING A CIRCLE OF CERTAINTY

An aspect of consciousness falls easily into a *circle of certainty*. This happens whenever consciousness becomes set in memory reality. Reality that is fixed cannot grow. Reality that is exclusive cannot include that which is excluded.

The *defense-control mechanism* acts as a dam holding back the possible flood that the sweep of awareness represents. Behind this dam, the waters of creative pressure build. Weaker dams are swept away when the pressure becomes too great but the *sweep of awareness* represented by the flowing water does not last long and the dam is easily rebuilt. Stronger dams, determined to maintain the flood of insight or *sweep of awareness,* break only after the exertion of great pressure. When this happens, the sweep of awareness is long and forceful. The aspect of consciousness may not be able to reconstruct a suitable barrier and in that case would have no control in the world of circumstance and material.

The maintainer aspect of consciousness leaves much of the dam construction to the organizer aspect. Having decided, in its reality, that it is incapable of, or does not want to be bothered with, reality creation, the maintainer aspect looks to the organizer aspect for declarations of "truth". By doing this the maintainer aspect allows the organizer aspect to declare the dimensions of its *circle of certainty.*

The organizer aspect of Mind declares for the maintainer aspect of Mind, that which is to be excluded and that which is to be included. Thus social and organizational definition is decided. These definitions are further enhanced and enforced by rules and regulations. The primary purpose of rule is to support and create comfort for those aspects of the organization with a more inclusive reality, by protecting them from those aspects of the organization with a more exclusive reality, and, from the influence of other organizations. The secondary purpose is to inhibit extension which has no regard for the purposes of the organization.

The organizational aspect itself may or may not be bound by the rules and regulations that it has declared. The *mental arrangement* here is somewhat different and more inclusive that the *mental arrangement* that has been declared for the maintainer aspect. It allows an investigatory freedom that can enhance the organization and its system of governance. This may, and, in more progressive systems, does, include input from the extender aspect. Organization is cautious, though, that the circle of certainty is maintained.

The extender aspect is cautious of "falling into" a *circle of certainty.* Knowing it to be a bane to extension, the extender aspect of Mind sees the *circle of certainty* to be temporary and dispensable. The extending aspect does use the circle, though, as a place of stability from which to extend. As extension takes place, the extending aspect creates stability at new levels of awareness, always relinquishing the now familiar circle, in order to stay in a *power spiral* of heightened awareness.

CAUSING A PORTAL OF PERCEPTION

Usually *portals of perception* are caused by the interaction of consciousness in the conditional world. Whenever the reality that is held dear does not prove to be an effective means of evaluating and stabilizing circumstances, a *portal of perception* occurs. This is the crack in the dam of the *defense-control mechanism.* The aspect of consciousness must then repair and reinforce the area that is cracked or the *sweep of awareness* will break through washing all barriers away.

The aspect of Mind that maintains and the aspect of Mind that organizes try to keep the *sweep of awareness* from happening by building and reinforcing formidable barriers that cannot be easily breached. A *portal of perception* could destroy their reality and nullify the investment that was made in its creation.

The aspect of Mind that extends does not develop, or rely heavily on, the *defense-control mechanism.* This allows reality to flow more freely as it is being continually refreshed with new insights and flowing with awareness in a *power spiral.*

When the extending aspect becomes mired in mediocrity and ordinariness, *the adventure quotient* becomes unbalanced creating a pressure that demands action. At this time the extending aspect finds the means to break *the circle of certainty* and experience *the sweep of awareness.*

Usually, the means used by the extender aspect to open a *portal of perception* are not acceptable organizationally and many times are in defiance of organizational decision. Since the organizational aspect of Mind establishes that which will cause a *circle of certainty* and keep a *portal of perception* from happening, that which will cause a *portal of perception* is held in disfavor or outlawed.

Sometimes the extender aspect throws itself into "death-defying" situations. Sometimes it meditates, relaxing the *defense-control mechanism.* Sometimes it finds and uses substances that will alter the *mental arrangement.* Sometimes it defies all that it "knows to be true". In any case, it risks the reality that it now holds in order to approach greater reality and understanding.

In doing this, the extending aspect finds reward. Each

risk of reality and subsequent survival with increased awareness encourages the extending aspect to take further risks. For the extending aspect there is no right or wrong, only the need to risk and grow more aware through defying some "supposed" limitation and establishing a new frontier.

Sometimes this works to the benefit of the organization and sometimes to its detriment. Usually the organizational aspect, in trying to protect the *circle of certainty,* views all new expression as being to its detriment until it is proven beneficial. This is one of the first barriers the extending aspect recognizes and overcomes by realizing that the purpose of most organizational expression is to create a *circle of certainty* and comfort.

THE LAW OF LIMITS

In a very real way, the aspect of Mind that extends is a *limit finder.* That is, this aspect never knows when it will try to defy some limit and as a result lose its ability to act in the world of material and circumstance. In doing so, the extending aspect demonstrates to the organizational and maintainer aspects that a limit does indeed exist and they become more cautious, using this information in their *circle of certainty.*

Limits in the conditional world are rediscovered continually by the extending aspect as it tries the "supposed" limits over and over. Conditions are subject to change. What was a limit yesterday may not be a limit tomorrow. All limits are probed by Mind through Its extending aspect to ascertain if they are extant.

Within the organization the proposed limits are probed also. Only those found to be true and continuous are heeded. Others that prove to be faulty and easily breached are ignored. The aspect of Mind that is extending demonstrates to the organization that it must either re-inforce these barriers or it must set them aside.

Consciousness is always reaching forward through its many aspects, surpassing limitations and recognizing new frontiers. Through its extending aspect it finds its way around all the barriers of the world of material and circumstance. Like water, it moves until it reaches a barrier; then it pools and expands until it either finds another avenue to flow, overflows or breaks the dam.

Consciousness has no concern for the consequences of this action. Acting from the "Law of Limits" when the limit is formidable and hampering The Creation, Mind acts through more extending aspects to breach the limit.

The aspect of Mind that is organizational, knowing this, sets up means of releasing creative pressure without jeopardizing the *circle of certainty.* The organizational aspect knows that if pressure is not released in favorable way that it will be released in an unfavorable way. Recognizing and indulging the extending aspect, it endeavors to turn the direction of extension into something organizationally useful or, failing that, something creatively ineffective.

The organizational aspect of Mind sees itself as giving direction to creative extension. This keeps the extension from being haphazard or redundant. Without the organizational aspect, extension would take place purposelessly. With it, the organization and all concerned "prosper". (This word only has meaning organizationally and is defined for purposes of social motivation.)

There is no conflict between Mind and Its aspects. What seems, at times, to be conflict is merely Mind adjusting to act in a different way in order to breach some barrier in the world of material and circumstance.

Maintainer aspects, incapable of making changes and

having a fixed reality that is no longer relevant, see conflict and must act within their reality to bring that which is different into line with the reality they have created.

The organizational aspect may or may not recognize the validity of the shift of Mind. This depends on the amount of investment there is in the familiar reality. The greater the investment, the greater will be the barrier against the opening of a portal of perception and any subsequent change in the circle of certainty.

When the organizational aspect recognizes the shift through the operation of its extending aspects and creates an avenue through which new insight and expression can flow, gradually changing the *circle of certainty,* the organization may survive the shift and continue to be *effectively creative.*

When the organizational aspect fails to recognize the shift or, recognizing it, ignores the shift, because of decisions in its *defense-control mechanism,* it becomes *creatively defective.* (Here, *creatively defective* organization is balanced by other equally defective organization. What one affirms, the other denies and visa-versa.)

UNIVERSAL BALANCE
or THE BALANCED UNIVERSE

The Universe, being undifferentiated, is always in balance. The decisions or actions of its aspects have no effect on this balance. All effects of the creation are counterbalanced each against another, maintaining equilibrium, and the keeping The Universe constant. That which appears to change is not **The Great Reality** but the lesser reality suggested by an aspect of consciousness in the world of material and circumstances.

Mind maintains balance by creation of alternates through Its aspects. Decisions to declare anything within

The Totality Of Being is a decision to declare its alternative. In the world of material and circumstance an aspect of consciousness does not recognize that the action that it takes is counterbalanced by the action of another aspect of consciousness. Consequently, the aspects often witness imbalance, conflict and disorder. To witness harmony and order, or conflict and disorder is a matter of choice.

THE TERMITE PRINCIPLE (This section is written in the language of the world of material and circumstance. This feature is not recognizable in the Reality of Mind.)
Everything will return to its natural state,
no matter what you try to do to prevent it.
There is a natural flow to the comings and goings of the material world. Consciousness that knows this flow and lives with it has no fear, for it knows that it is part of and involved in **Something Infinitely Greater.** In knowing this, it knows **Its Continuity and Timelessness.**

It is only consciousness that sees itself as separate and apart that experiences or needs to experience fear. That is its means of maintaining its separation and, therefore, what it considers itself to be. Identifying with that which is material and operating in a circumstantial world, it spends its time creating defectively, looking only for means to sustain or recreate itself.

Separated consciousness forgets that, in the world of material and circumstance, construction of one thing is always destruction of another. Consequently, there is never a change in Reality, only a change in form. Form is always changing, never the same from one moment to the next.

A seed changes elements from the earth, air and sun creating a special order so that these elements become a tree. The tree grows changing the original molecular structure into leaves, fruit and seeds. The fruit is destroyed by being eaten to construct a person. The person is part of the process and is always materially destroyed becoming part of and involved in that which all life is part of and involved in, **The Cycle of Being.**

Usually we look at the constructive side, at least from our viewpoint, of **The Cycle of Being.** We proclaim that side good because it seems to suit our purposes. We proclaim the destructive side, that which would destroy our separation and return us to what we really are and have always have been, to be bad. By doing this we seek to protect ourselves and sustain that which we consider ourselves to be.

If we use the termite as a symbol for those forces in nature that we consider destructive, we can see the necessity for the existence of those forces. In relaxing our hold on a reality of separation and fear, we can begin to view a greater, more inclusive reality.

The termite's only purpose, it would appear, is to tear down wood fiber, reducing it to elemental ingredients, so that the forest can regrow. You could see the termite as, "The living embodiment of those forces in nature which tend to return things to their natural state."

Without the termite, the forest would have difficulty producing new growth. There are other factors that tear down wood fiber, too, but none so evident as the termite. Without wood there would be no termite. Without the termite the forest would suffer.

Everything in nature has its destructive side to keep everything in harmony and balance. When something moves too far one way, the counterbalance which is seen as destructive moves an equal distance in the other.

Since the aspect of Mind which is human consciousness, is capable of construction that is not easily dismantled by other forces in nature, the ability and predisposition to destroy has also been assigned to human consciousness. The greater the structure, the greater its underlying force for destruction.

But, just as every tree has its time for growing, fruiting and decaying, so do the structures of human consciousness. While they are flowering, fruiting and healthy, they cannot be attacked by the termite of destruction. Only when they have aged and are no longer serving a useful purpose are they subject to destruction from the attack of their negative counterpart.

In the world of material and circumstance, many organizations are like trees that no longer bear fruit because their trunks will no longer carry the sap which gives sustainence and guarantees their survival to the leaves. They wither and are dead but yet remain standing because of their many years of investment in structure.

It is then that the *termite of transition* appears and the defense system of the organization stiffens in opposition, trying to hide the fact of its death. Using every means possible to keep its fibers intact, it constructs a defense-control system that will not allow doubt or any expression that is not common language. It arms itself against that from which it considers itself separate.

Any organization which no longer has strength of purpose and has become ineffective cannot retain its identity any more than the tree that no longer delivers fruit. If it is not destroyed from the inside, as the *adventure quotient* demands release, it will be from the outside, as the termite of transition gnaws away its useless fibers. But, then, the essence of it is contained in the seeds it has delivered and it is involved in all new thought and new expression.

Any organization which has strength of purpose is effective and cannot be harmed by doubt or other expression. Each expression that is not self-contradictory, and each new experience, only add to its stature and health. This too will serve its time and pass away. Until then, so long as the adventure quotient is allowed release and the expression remains inclusive, the organization will flourish and its members prosper in that which they hold important.

The termite of transition is always about, ready and waiting to devour doctrine that is not effective or no longer comes from Truth and reduce it to its elemental form. This represents the destruction of old form and the construction of new form that is present in all manifestations of Mind.

Chapter IX

ARRANGING THE WORLD

Every statement of our beginnings has been formed by witnessing the world of material and circumstance, constructing a mental model that declares the how and why of things, and offering the resulting expression as an explanation. As we become more cognizant of early developments, we are better able to express. Unfortunately, any new expression runs into what has been previously expressed and is now being recited. There is usually a conflict between the new, more relevant expression, and the old expression which is obsolete and not in concert with the circumstances or the language of the present age.

This chapter is directed to you, whatever you consider yourself to be. It is for you, the writer of this material, for you, the reader of this material, for you, who hear(s) this material, for you, who recognizes the existence of this material and either uses it or avoids it, and for you, who have no realization of this material's existence.

The pronoun, you, is used throughout this chapter to designate that aspect of consciousness which is processing this information in order to become more aware of its own operation and, therefore, its possibilities. It can be replaced by any other pronoun that you may decide to use to divide, separate and distinguish aspects of Reality. This is inclusive of, but not limited to I, me, mine, you, your, yours, he, him, his, she, her, hers, along with their plural forms, and whosoever or whomsoever, and all varieties of pronouns in different cants and languages.

Do not be deluded by your ability to separate yourself from "others" and decide that this material is for them and is not applicable to you or your situation. Do not persuade yourself that you are already an enlightened being and could gain nothing by witnessing life from another viewpoint. In accepting the validity of this material you will find release, growth and empowerment. In deciding that it has no value and avoiding the essential guidance of this expression you will have chosen to remain blind to your possibility and your own true nature. You are that which decides and your decisions are honored by **Your Greater Self.**

If you choose to disregard all or any part of this material, that is your decision. There is no right or wrong choice. If you wish to make the journey of life without a map or with little torn slips of paper assembled in desperation in moments of panic, it may be more exhilarating and adventurous. The awareness that you may not survive if you do not grasp **The Essential Truth of Your Being** may be what you need in order to gain the understanding that is presented here. There is a deeper part of you which knows what to investigate and what to ignore.

Whether you decide to accept or ignore this material, you must realize what is being offered. When you realize what is being offered, your decision comes from awareness and not from blindness. Your acceptance or rejection of this material is, then, one of knowledgeable interest and not one of fear.

What is being offered to you is a map. This map is accurate, detailed and reliable. Depending on the degree to which you accept its accuracy and how you use it, it will show you how to get from "point A to point B" for your personal growth, your spiritual development or just for the adventure of going from "point A to point B."

The intention, herein, is not to show you where you are. That is for you to decide. It is rather to show you a wide variety of *mental arrangements,* how they are achieved and how they are maintained, so that you may better recognize where you are now, better decide where you want to be, and better select the route by which you can transport yourself to that mental location. Of course, if you do not like where you are, this metaphysical map will help you see how you got there so that you can redecide the path along which you are traveling. Also, if you do not like the direction in which you are headed, this will help you pick a new direction that is equally interesting, yet not so cluttered with conflict.

Remember, also, that the particulars of your unique *mental arrangement* are indistinct to consciousness that does not know separation or knows less separation than you experience in your reality. Hence, the greater, more inclusive consciousness, can only suggest the divisions that you may have made, the ideas you hold important and the conflicts you have created within your *mental arrangement.* It is up to you to recognize what is valid and applicable in your life situation. It is your responsibility to use the information that you find relevant and modify your *mental arrangement* to become more creatively effective.

The order of illustration, in this study, begins at the lowest point in the "canyon of conceit", the level of maximum separation, and proceeds through the various participatory levels of consciousness until it reaches the point of maximum inclusion and maximum awareness, **The Universal Self.**

Plateau One:
TOTAL ISOLATION AND DETACHMENT
This is the maximum concentration or "psychosis". If you were at this level, you would not be reading this material, unless you have become a fanatic about this particular expression to the exclusion of all other possibilities. If

you feel that this or another expression is the complete answer to all questions and have decided to set aside all other expressions of a similar or different nature, keeping before you only selected truths you have realized in reading and studying this or other material, you are a saint (the blind follower of a certain creed). Otherwise, you are a heathen or infidel (one who sees fault in all creed and expression presented by others).

It does not matter what anyone else says or does; no one can sway you from your belief. You do not think about what anyone else says, because you "know the truth". You have your entire concentration on what you are doing and are able to do it extremely well, not caring whether anyone else agrees or disagrees.

You consider yourself unique, separate and independent from anything you witness, perhaps having been spawned on some other planet or through some extraordinary circumstance. You know yourself to be unlike anything you witness, even the body you operate. Because you have no fear, you are capable of performing feats that no one else can. You use the body as a tool, adjusting it for optimum operation and using it to control those who would stand in your way.

What happens to your body is of no concern because you know that you are not your body. Being completely disassociated from the body which you operate, you have no fear of death and you are able to express this in your deeds.

Being deep within the *canyon of conceit,* you see only the path you have chosen and have armed yourself to overcome the situations that might occur as you grope into the darkened passages of the world of material and circumstance. Many times, you see yourself as the wealth or power that you have accumulated. When you are deprived of these things that you have made important, you feel that you are deprived of life. You sometimes destroy the body with which you work because you feel that it has failed you in your ambitious pursuits.

This is the *mental arrangement* you have chosen to use. You have set up barriers against suggested changes to this arrangement. In your *defense-control mechanism,* you have a system of automatic reactions that protects you from the influence of what you see as separate and different.

Because of your blindness to conditions and your unwillingness to be influenced, you find that much of the time you are forced to use violent reactions to control your world. When you are able to be alone and have the wherewithal to follow your interests, you have no problem; you master each challenge as it occurs.

When you are thwarted in your desires by conditions or by "others", you use anger, hostility, deceit, prevarication and violence. Since you see everything you consider as not yourself, you lie to yourself, building a *mental arrangement* of fabrication as a bulwark.

Because of your unwillingness to change your *mental arrangement,* you always see that which you feel separate from, and superior to, as being at fault. You have arranged reality in such a way that any suggestion of your being at fault will trigger your *defense-control mechanism* and send you into a tirade.

Since you have blocked all channels through which change may occur in order to maintain your *mental arrangement,* you are unable to change your *mental arrangement.* You do not realize that you have chosen a certain path at the very bottom of the *canyon of conceit,* and that you have decided to be where you are and to do what you are doing. You see it all as someone or something else's fault and someone or something else's decision. When you run into conflict along the path you have chosen, you think only of destroying that which appears to be in your way and causing the conflict.

When you intercept conflict along your path, your only course of action is to destroy that which you see as the cause of conflict before it destroys you. Since you have so few alternative methods of control, you are severely limited but make good use of the methods that you have, intimidating, criticizing, slandering, abusing or physically disabling those with whom you find yourself in conflict.

Giving all your power to others in conflict situations by seeing them as the cause of the disagreement, you fight them because you see them as depriving you of power. Excluding others, you fight them because you feel excluded. When you run into an insurmountable conflict that you have no means of controlling, you do not realize that you are literally "out of control" because you have no means of making that measurement with the "yardstick" you possess.

You have no means of evaluating your *mental arrangement* and, therefore, no means of changing it. The only way that you can advance to a more inclusive arrangement is through the intercession of another who operates at a greater level of consciousness, finds your situation interesting and challenging, and is willing to be instrumental in your development of *a more inclusive mental arrangement.*

Plateau Two:
THE SEPARATED INDIVIDUAL
There is a thin dividing line between Level One, "Psychosis," and Level Two, "Neurosis." At Level Two, you concern yourself more with the body. You see yourself as being beautiful or ugly, handsome or homely, attractive

or repulsive. You know yourself to be separate from others and from the circumstances that you encounter. Your world consists of comparisons of what you see as you (your body) to what you see as not you (the bodies of others).

You are now concerned with what others think of you and you try to control your world by causing them to think well of you. When they do, you are delighted and delightful, rewarding them with praise and favors. When they don't you become irritated, angry, and have "hurt feelings". You see them as the cause of your anger, your frustration and your misery.

You continually try out new ways of dressing, fixing your hair, building your body, and establishing a reputation to attract the opinions that you feel are helpful to you along the path you have selected near the bottom of the *canyon of conceit*. Because you have identified with the physical attributes of the body which you experience yourself as controlling, you worry over every aspect of its development and its recognition in the world you witness.

You have learned to be clever, witty, sarcastic, haughty and supercilious in your effort to control the world you witness. Sometimes you even become physically ill, have accidents and could even destroy your body in your effort to cause others to like you. These become alternative tools in your *defense-control mechanism* As you use these they become natural and you forget that you have chosen them.

Because of the reality you have created, you are terrified of "death" and will do anything to survive and gain power over those you see as enemies (anyone who may be capable of controlling you more than you control them). You have no concern for what happens in the world as long as you have your way. When you don't get your way, you look for those who are to blame. Your personal success or failure is of primary importance, anything and everything else is secondary.

Usually, there is no hereafter concept in your mental arrangement. You feel that you are entitled to live forever in the bodily form that you are familiar with and have made important. You spend much of your time trying to avoid "aging" and "death". When you do have a *hereafter concept,* it is one of continuing your personal separation and familiar reality, like the concept of personal reincarnation.

Socially, you seem adjusted to the circumstances of the conditional world (when things are going your way) but privately you writhe in fear that you will be "found out", lose your position or the influence you have on the conditional world that you have created.

Because you have made yourself small you must try to make yourself large in the sight and mind of others. You take credit for everything you can with which you have had any connection. If there is blame, you always try to find someone else who is responsible. You emphasize their faults and hide your own.

You recognize those at Level One consciousness. You know how to manipulate them but are wary of their propensity to see you as their enemy. You know that they may change their minds about whether you are helpful to them at any moment. Many times you find yourself in conflict with those at Level One and withdraw in order to keep the conflict from escalating into violence. You know that if violence erupts you will have to participate and that is not your desire. You have found ways of controlling the world you witness without being violent and only use violence as a last resort.

You have no ability to make adjustments of your *mental arrangement* because you take credit for every thing you think and, therefore, cannot accept that there can be any error in your thought system. When you feel you have "lost control", you search out someone who you feel is more adept in the world of material and circumstances. By doing this, you make adjustments to your *mental arrangement* but, then, you are quick to separate yourself from them when you feel that you are back in control of your situation. You cannot allow that they may be responsible for your improved understanding or more coherent behavior. For you to do so, in your *mental arrangement,* would be to lessen what you think yourself to be.

Plateau Three:
FAMILY, TEAM OR SMALL GROUP.

This is the third level of *fixed mental arrangement* or "Religious Non-Seeking." Here, you are not so interested in competing with others. You are more interested in being a member of a group. Your *mental arrangement* is that you are more than an individualized body, you are the family or group in which the body is participating.

You may have decided that this family group is bounded by biological lines, like bloodline or genetic code. You may have decided that this group is bounded by lines controlled by sporting or business rules. You may have decided that your family consists of others who have a similar *mental arrangement* to yours. Just as you have decided your individual identity at Level Two, here, you recognize those with whom you identify and know your involvement. You know that whatever happens to those with whom you identify happens to you.

You know the language of the family and are comfortable with it. You know that your family has secrets and expressions that may not be understood by those who are not family members. You can say outrageous things to other members and do outrageous things in their presence. They take insults from you that they would not tolerate from those they consider "outsiders."

Just as you drew lines to divide what you have decided is you at Level Two, so you create a boundary here to define what you consider to be family and not family. It is your decision and you know yourself to be your family. You have no consideration for a self that is separate and distinct from family. The family gives you definition and you give the family the power to decide your life's path.

You see the achievement of any family member as your achievement and the failure of any family member as your failure. At times you are helpful and encouraging to other members, being patient with them in their time of stress; at other times you are severely disapproving of the actions of other members, feeling that what they do makes you less.

You measure your family against other families, comparing their attributes to yours, competing with them and striving to make your family more powerful than theirs. You emphasize their faults while minimizing your own. You are cordial with them while trying to find better ways to improve ties within your own family.

You arrived at this level by making fewer divisions important than you considered important at Levels One and Two or by not realizing Level One and Two divisions in the first place. You maintain this level of consciousness by not recognizing or not accepting invitations that will cause you to feel separate from other family members.

Your mental arrangement as a family member is one of concern for other family members. There is an intermeshing relationship where you see yourself as involved in the family and nothing that happens can change that involvement. You know each other's wants and needs and you supply that which is necessary, taking from other families, if necessary, to do so.

Your hereafter concept at this level is one of reward, for doing that which enhances family or *punishment,* for doing that which depletes family. In the biological family, reward is being with one's more respected ancestors after "death" in an eternal Eden, Heaven or Utopia. For others, the reward of the hereafter is being with family members who no longer are embodied. Hereafter concepts differ slightly for each person, but there is enough similarity that the individuals do not feel threatened by the difference. The concept that you use is expressive of your decision to operate at this level. The more confined your concept is, the more confined your thinking is and the more confined your operation is.

You can descend to Levels One or Two in the *canyon of conceit* by deciding that you are different from other family members and making this idea of difference important. You can solidify this separation by ridiculing them for the differences you have created and use their reaction as the reason for your withdrawal from the relationship or familial situation. You may even be able to cause them to harm you physically and use this for the reason for breaking off the association.

Since it is downhill, descending in the *canyon of conceit* is easy. You only need to make a difference of opinion important and then escalate the disagreement. You can continue until you sense that you have sufficient evidence (whether this consists of insult, rejection, or physical abuse is up to you) and then log this information into your *defense control mechanism* to keep from returning to the same familial situation. By making the actions of someone else responsible for your decision to separate, you can successfully block the avenue of return.

While it is easy to descend into the canyon, it is difficult to ascend. If your *mental arrangement* requires the action of another before you can return to the family level, you have disempowered yourself and must remain at a lower level of consciousness until such action takes place. You may, however, come to Level Three consciousness in a different family or relationship circumstance. If you do not realize how you separated yourself from others before and descended to a lower level of consciousness, you will probably create the same condition in your new relationship. Eventually, you will either learn how to maintain your balance at the family level or you will resign yourself to operation at Level One or Two.

To move from a lower, more exclusive, mental arrangement to a higher, more inclusive, mental arrangement, you must have, within the present mental arrangement, a method of transformation. This serves to counteract the automatic reaction that you have logged into the *defense control mechanism.* The more you move from the lesser to the *greater mental arrangement,* the more adept you become. When you learn to master circumstance instead of reacting to it, you recognize invitations to automatic reaction, and are more able to move from one level of consciousness to another.

The initial rising to a greater level of consciousness is more difficult, since you have not experienced operation at that level. One of the difficulties is that other family members are usually concerned about how your change of consciousness will effect the family group. If they have not experienced operation at a greater level, they have no ability to measure your growth. It may be that all they can see is that you have changed. They, then, must decide whether you are still a family member or whether you may be a threat to the family group.

When you are going through a transformation (a change of levels), family members are alert to any sign that you may now be an "outsider." This has to be taken into consideration and you may need to reassure them that what you are experiencing will enhance, rather than deplete, them at the family level. Even so, if they are holding a hard family line and you recognize the commonness between your family and the family of others, holding it more important than the difference, you may be rejected and seen as being on the other side of the dividing line that they have drawn.

When this happens, you are forced to decide whether to forgo transformation and remain at the family level of consciousness or forgo the family *mental arrangement* and allow the transformation to take place. This is a very difficult place of decision. There are few that allow this change of consciousness to take place. Most are afraid of losing their niche in the family *circle of certainty*.

There are a few difficulties associated with your possible change of levels. Some of those at family level of consciousness have experienced the discomfort of intercepting the transformation possibility and have opted to remain at Level Three. They feel that they must prevent you from experiencing this discomfort "for your own good". Others are concerned that you will not be there when they need you. This is a viable concern at family level and it is the reason many decide to operate at the family level rather than at the more separate levels. Additionally, since those who are at family level operate from a *fixed mental arrangement* of a certain religious or ethnic persuasion, they are afraid that you will break their *circle of certainty* and cause them to reflect on their own operation.

Another problem is that it is at the family level that you find the greatest concentration of humanity. Although you may operate at other levels of consciousness, this is the level from which you usually operate. Here, you have *the stability of a fixed mental arrangement* and are among others like yourself who have decided to operate from this amount of separation. There is a great amount of pressure to cause you to stay at this level. Those who are not at this level seem weird. You and those with whom you associate are cautious of them, dealing with them only in emergencies. At the same time, many of these outsiders are respected and you turn to them for help.

These are factors that enter into any transformation of consciousness. When rising to a greater level, there are always restraining factors at the level you are leaving that you must overcome. *If you cannot overcome the restraints present at lesser, more exclusive, levels of consciousness, you cannot arrive at a greater, more inclusive level.*

Plateau Four:
ORGANIZATION, LARGE GROUP
You witness enough of the operation of other families to know that the family level is the backbone of the system, "the salt of the earth.." Without their operation any system would fail and fall apart. You realize, also, that most of those acting at Levels One and Two are detrimental to any system. Because of their inattention to system process, or, possibly worse, their scoffing at system process, they are the "trouble makers."

These realizations cause you to act as "clergy" in the "Participatory Levels of Consciousness." Your overview has increased, causing you to become more inclusive in your thoughts and actions. Now you recognize that divisions between families are not important. What is important is the cooperation of families with families. You see persuading those operating at Levels One and Two to operate at Level Three and bringing the Level Three families into harmony as your life's purpose.

Using the words of others who have preceeded you, you become evangelistic. You use every means at your disposal to influence and persuade others to follow you and give you their power so that you can "create a better world" for them. Sometimes you are intimidating, sometimes threatening, sometimes coercive, sometimes caring and sometimes loving, but you always see it as being for the good of those you influence.

You learn quickly how to control others and build a power structure. Using words and writings that are already held in reverence by those you would influence, you make them more powerful, attributing them to beings of mysticism and mythology. Sometimes, you say that these are the words of XXX, the highest being and power imaginable. You proclaim other expressions erroneous and mythological and yours true and indisputable. In doing so you draw dividing lines between the expression you promulgate and the expressions promulgated by others.

Knowing your followers' propensity to concern themselves with the hereafter, you proclaim that unless they heed your words and follow your teachings, which you couch in the more accepted scriptural language, they are doomed for eternity. (In a very real way you are right, but not because they do not heed the words you promulgate as "truth". They, as you, are doomed by the divisions you make and hold important and by ignorance of **Your Essential Being.**)

At times you succumb to invitations to operate at lower levels of consciousness, taking credit for your accomplishments and using the power you have been entrusted with unwisely. When this happens, you become more concerned about your possible loss of power than about your purpose and function. Instead of helping others rise to a higher level of consciousness, you condemn them for operating at the level they have chosen. You become more interested in controlling others than in helping them realize their potential. All scripture you profess to believe becomes twisted for this end. Through use of it you seek to subdivide Reality creating your own petty empire.

When you are "on purpose" and acting in accordance with *Your Inner Knowledge Which Knows No Division,* you aid others in approaching a greater understanding of their own operation. In doing this you experience the real reward, the reward of Knowledge.

You can stay at this level, reciting scripture and teaching others to recite scripture, never being quite aware of what it means or why you have made it important. In doing so, you will never become aware of **The Reality That Brings All Manifestations Into Being**. You will only be aware that by declarations of right and wrong you can cause those at lesser levels of consciousness to do your bidding and come to you for answers.

You have become the authority in their lives. You can either use this power to help them climb to a higher level in the *canyon of conceit* or you can use it to keep them at lesser levels of conscious awareness so that you can indulge in your control of them. This is the basic choice you make as clergy. Through this choice, you either deny the greater self in which you participate (the name that you give it is unimportant), or you honor the greater self. It is through this decision that you either descend to a lower level of consciousness or rise to a higher level.

When you make the name you have given to **The Greater Self** more important than the name someone else has given to **The Greater Self**, or you have declared a certain aspect of **The Greater Self** more important than another aspect of **The Greater Self**, you confine yourself to the level of clergy. It is your decision and your definition that prevents you from recognizing your greatness. You may think that having a large following and being able to wield power makes you great. There are many in your churches, temples, clubhouses, tabernacles and schools who are greater than you. Greatness is the result of thinking and acting inclusively. That which you exclude you have declared to be not involved in **The Greater Self.** By thinking so, you diminish greatness. By recognizing **The Union of All Existence,** you realize greatness.

Plateau Five:
NATION, TERRITORIAL, LINGUAL AND
ECONOMIC BOUNDARIES
This is the level at which one begins to catch a glimpse of Truth. It is here that you are a "religious seeker". You are at this level because you now realize that the mystical boundaries defined by clergy are not real. You realize that **The Greater Self** is given many names by many organizations. You know, too, that all these organizations or "religions" fail to recognize that what empowers them is the same reality even though they name it differently.

The only divisions you have at this level are those of physical placement, language and economic system. Because you operate from a certain physical location with boundaries set by governmental decision, or speak a certain language, or operate within a certain economic system, you see other places, languages or economic systems as being faulty. (Sometimes this division is also misconstrued as skin pigmentation.)

Here, even though you see the similarity of organizations and religions, you still give importance to these other divisions. You are either working to reduce the tension created here or you are working to increase this tension.

Sometimes, "religious" difference is a factor here, too. When it is, there is a great increase in the amount of conflict that can be generated. Operation is best at this level when you do not know which "religion" is superior. When the idea of "religious" superiority enters, you tend to justify the most heinous actions against that from which you have decided you are separate and to which you have decided you are superior.

Your reality, here, as it is at all levels, is the consequence of the divisions you have made and hold important. To operate at this level, you have recognized the superficiality of "religious" beliefs and that, while reducing conflict at Levels One, Two and Three, they cause greater conflict at Level Four. Now, you see territorial, language and economic differences as being natural and the only important factors that separate humanity. Pride in the differences you see between your nation and other nations keeps you at this level.

Knowing this, you either hold fast to these boundaries, protecting your territory, your people and your economic system, or you search for solutions that will minimize these differences. This is your calling at this level of consciousness. As at all levels, it is one of either amplifying the differences you have realized or seeing beyond these differences to reach the common ground.

Since Mind does not know these differences, one way leads to conflict, misunderstanding and war, while the other way leads to harmonious creation, awareness and peace. By choosing well here, you progress to the next level of understanding.

Sometimes you decide not to choose war, and you try to choose peace as an alternative. What you do not realize is that war and peace are not options, they are conditions that arise in the material world from choosing divisions and holding them important. When the importance of these arbitrary divisions is relaxed, peace is assured. So long as these importances are held before the window of mind, conflict is assured. Because reality is decided in consciousness in opposing pairs, to make the idea of peace important is to make the idea of war equally important.

Plateau Six:
HUMANITY, THE REFLECTIVE ASPECT
This is the realm of the "philosopher", one who questions the presumptions of social process and of nations. Seeing all human divisions as arbitrarily imposed on the canvas of social order, you experiment with different ways these divisions can be arranged, the amount of importance to be accorded to each, and the consequences of these decisions.

Now, through travel, you have seen the the ridiculousness of territorial boundaries. Through interaction with other societies, speaking in other tongues you realize that, for the most part, they, like you, wish only to have the freedom to be creatively effective and to live their lives in harmony. You have traded enough with those in distant lands to know that they are not motivated by greed. They wish only to have the wherewithal to fulfill their life's purpose. To have less is disempowering; to have more is confining. Realizing how small is their need, you willingly share your wealth and your time.

From here, you look back at that insignificant self that you thought was so important at lesser levels of consciousness and laugh at the person you once thought you were, at the world you once thought was real, and at the actions you once took at times of anguish, exhilaration, fear and disappointment. You now see that they were all the result of the way you had arranged reality and you know that any suffering you may have experienced in human interaction was caused by your misunderstanding of your true nature and the true nature of others.

You are now human, one with all of humanity, and that is enough. To desire to be special is to be less and to desire to be better is to be worse. Realizing this, you aid **The Creative Process** wherever you can, in whatever capacity you are allowed. For the first time you are beginning to feel really alive.

You realize that you are operative at every level, in every capacity. You no longer have to fight for space or recognition because you see yourself in every face, in every body, and in every action that you intercept. You interact with yourself at all levels of your being, knowing that it is you who is learning and doing so that you may continue your growth and enhance your understanding.

You realize that you can descend to any level by making the divisions established at that level important. You witness the self, which you previously thought of as others, at the lower levels of consciousness and experience the divisions that you (they) have made in order to experience the anger, frustration, exhilaration and disappointment that you (they) have chosen to experience through your (their) choice of divisions. Wherever possible, you help yourself (them) with the lesson you (they) have chosen to learn. You make no judgment, for they are you. You take no credit, for you are they.

Pride in the differences you see between your human self and other creatures keeps you at this level of consciousness. Because of your ability to extend beyond where they are, you enjoy using them at your discretion for your purposes. Thinking them outside of the circle of inclusion you have drawn, you neglect them except where you feel that it benefits humanity.

Plateau Seven:
ANIMAL, THE FREEDOM OF MOVEMENT

At this level you are "spiritually communicative", knowing the divisions that you make in other *mental arrangements* that bring pain and suffering to yourself as a separate individual and to yourself in the form of all other creatures. You ponder this realization, knowing your ability to change the importance you attach to the divisions that you establish. You still feel the need to explain this and encourage the self you see in other forms to recognize its greatness.

You recognize that you are and have always been an animal, a creature that is capable of horizontal movement upon the earth's crust or vertical movement in the air and oceans. You now relax the ideas that keep you separate from the other creatures of the earth. The idea, that you have the ability to reflect on your mental process and they do not, becomes less important than the infinite similarities and the realization that you are an outgrowth of **The Natural Process** that brought them into existence.

You rediscover your animal self and are amazed at the many possibilities that now flow before your mind's eye. You realize that you have hidden these wonders behind ideas of separation and superiority. Now, you are fascinated by these many aspects of yourself that you witness in every creature that you intercept. You realize, also, that you have always been trying to bring this to your conscious attention, in spite of the many "religious" beliefs that declared your separation. Now you know that you have found **True Religion**, the realization that you are not really separate from the animals of the world.

For some time, you protect the creatures of the world from abuse and from extinction, knowing that in protect-

143

ing them you are protecting yourself. You realize yourself as an innocent child, no longer able to understand the madness that persuades itself of its superiority and its "dominion." You know the divisions that you must imply to hold that *mental arrangement* and you avoid any invitation that would lead you in that direction. But, still, you understand yourself (them) making that decision. You cannot sit in judgment on or fear that which you know to be yourself.

Plateau Eight:
LIVING, THE AWARENESS OF GROWTH AND CHANGE

You are at the realm of conscious awareness, "spiritually non-communicative", where you now realize the greater extent of what you are. Just as an infant has made no distinctions about its nature, so it is that you now realize that you are more than the human, animal self, that you were taught to recognize yourself as and make important.

It dawns upon your consciousness that, in order to be a mobile creature you must feed on that which is rooted to the earth. Without the plants, the animal could not exist. In recognizing this, you know your continuity with all life forms and realize that all life is a part of you and you have no existence separate from it. You experience exhilaration and peace in this realization and have no desire other than to live in communion with nature.

You know now that you were never really apart from nature and that, at times, you pretended a separation that did not exist. There were many things you learned in your pretense and at times you enjoy reviewing the lessons. You have no need to share these insights, though, because you know that all life has this knowledge and all creatures are involved in this divine interplay.

Plateau Nine:
COSMIC CONSCIOUSNESS, UNIVERSAL AWARENESS

This is the level of "Undifferentiated Spirit". Now, ideas of life and death have lost their importance. You recognize that there is no life without the air which you breath, which, until this time, you have classified as non-living. You realize that the dividing line between you (whatever that is) and the air is arbitrary. It is not real nor has it ever been. You cannot define exactly where what you have called inert matter becomes vegetable, or where vegetable becomes you. This is the seat from which you operate as a *Person of Knowledge.*

You realize that it has all been a game, all the naming and divisions were merely a dream that You had in the quiet of eternity. You know that You have dreamed this dream before and that You will dream it again. But each time You fall asleep and step into the dream, it becomes more beautiful and more coherent. In the dream, You play many roles in many ways and You experience the pleasure of knowing that You are playing in each role better than You have ever played before. You applaud Yourself, encouraging all Your aspects to their greatest performance.

REALIZATIONS:

You and I select the level from which we choose to operate. We do so by deciding what differences we see and classifying them with the amount of importance we desire.

We are operative at all levels of consciousness, but we tend to prefer a certain level over the others. Often we forget that this was and is our choice. At the lower levels of con-

sciousness we tend to blame this on others. At the higher levels we realize that there are no "others".

The world we witness is the result of the mental arrangement at the level from which we have chosen to operate. We see "others" through our individualized system of divisions. Often we tend to blame them for the way we have chosen to create them in our system of divisions and importances. When you or I choose to witness life from the greater inclusion of higher consciousness levels, all tendency to blame disappears. It is then that we witness the perfection of the circumstance and know the right action that is the fulfillment of our purpose in the conditional world.

Every time we find someone or something to blame, we give away our power and descend to a lower level of operation, declaring something from which we are separate. When we know ourselves to be responsible for the circumstance we are witnessing, we rise to a higher level. Here, seeing more, we realize a greater number of alternative actions that we can take to remedy the circumstance or prevent its recurrence.

Sometimes you and I have difficulty communicating because we have chosen to operate from different levels. When we are at the same level of consciousness, we have no problem communicating even though we may be communicating in conflict because of the differences we have each chosen to declare important. Behind the facade, we know our love for each other, for, at a greater level of consciousness, we know that our divisions are not real and that we are not really separate.

EPILOGUE

Every age has an expression with which it establishes identity. By means of such expression its growth and development are directed. By means of the same expression, its limits are defined.

Governing bodies that occur within a certain age are stabilized by the scripture they hold to be true. Through use of this scripture, the possibilities of those governed are either enhanced or limited. The more exclusive the expression is, the more limited the possibilities are.

Every age, also, has those individuals who see beyond the limits set by the governing bodies, recognizing the flaws that create conflict and cause The Creation to happen ineffectively. Knowing truth, they are caused to react. Knowing necessity, they are caused to speak. During their embodiment, they are largely misunderstood because they are not in concert with the present expression of the government and of those governed.

In the society of their forefathers, they speak at risk. They must say what needs to be said even though they know that, within the confines of the present social mental arrangement, it will be misunderstood.

A person of knowledge does not speak for the present generation. The present generation always operates from a past expression. The message is never for this world (this mental arrangement) but for the next (the mental arrangement of the dawning age).

Few people receive the message. Most do not realize a message has been delivered. Others hear it through the filter of their *mental arrangement,* bringing to it the distortion of their preconception. Many recognize the truth and validity of what is said but shy away because of personal or social concerns. Still others become openly hostile because in their heart of hearts they know that the message will change their lives forever.

The few that receive the message do so because they realize that what is being said is true and beneficial. Being open-minded, they have dedicated themselves to following Truth wherever it might lead. Being aware, they recognize Truth and gladly drink it in, knowing it to be the expression of their soul. Being courageous, they express the message, encouraging others to recognize its truth and beauty.

You and I are the cause of the reality we witness. When we follow Truth, wherever it may come from and wherever it may lead, we reduce the conflict in our reality. Rising above the contradictions inherent in mental arrangements at lower levels of consciousness, we approach that Great Understanding that sees purpose in all that is observed. It is from here that we make our decisions about the role we are to play in the world of material and circumstance.

At this time, humanity, for a large part, is in the *Eighth Season of Human Development.* We have already passed through the point of maximum psychosis, where the idea of our complete separation from all that we witness was popular. We have overcome the neurosis where we thought in terms of keeping our bodies alive forever. We have recognized the importance of family ties. We have found that being involved in organization is empowering. We now realize that national might invites its own opposition and that war, as a creative process, is obsolete.

It is beginning to dawn upon us that we are not separate from, superior to, and better than the other creatures of the earth. Because of pollution, we are beginning to realize that we are not separate from the air we breath, the food we eat and the water we drink.

We can no longer afford a sloppy mental arrangement that invites conflict and misunderstanding. We cannot afford to have expressions that declare that we, because of our belief, are superior to and better than someone else or some other group. We cannot afford to pretend that we, because of our belief system are closer to "The Creator" than someone else or something else. Whether we survive the eighth season and continue into the harmony of the ninth and tenth is determined by decisions that we make now.

It is not a matter of persuading others to unite. It is a matter of realizing that **we are one.** It is not a matter of doing nothing about the conditions we observe. We must act. We have no choice in that. We do have a choice, though, of whether to act from the confusion of an exclusive mental arrangement or the awareness of a mental arrangement that is inclusive.

Among us are those who have already entered the ninth and tenth seasons. They reach down to encourage us, and give us support, even as we delude ourselves with our ideas of separation and superiority. When we allow ourselves, we are lifted higher in the *canyon of conceit.* They do not make demands, intimidate us, or threaten us with eternal damnation. Knowing us to be them, they are gentle and offer guidance, knowing that we must proceed at our own pace.

There are those, deeper than us in the canyon of conceit, who experience the confusion and conflict of the level at which they operate. We can condemn them for being there, laugh derisively at their actions, be fearful of them, avoid any contact with them, or gently bring them to an awareness of their greatness, knowing that they are us.

You and I are either separate or we are involved in one another, just as we are involved in the world we witness and The Universe that allows and encourages our existence. I accept that this is so and recognize my continuation in you. If you feel separate or are experiencing conflict, there are only the differences that you have declared important and the distance that you require to complete your understanding.

Appendix I

THE HIERARCHY OF AWARENESS

Level One: RECITATION
Small talk, avoidance of the unfamiliar. Narrow and confining, fixed reality. Separation from other fixed realities.

Level Two: MYSTERY
Fixed reality with a suggestion of the unknown. Expression of ideas heard but never witnessed or investigated. Recitation of the familiar plus recitation of ideas, conditions or suppositions encountered through hearsay but unfamiliar.

Level Three: INVESTIGATION
Reaching out for understanding of the unfamiliar. Operation from fixed, postnatal, beliefs maintained. The loss of fear of that which seems different or difficult.

Level Four: ALTERNATION
Recognition and acceptance of the reliability of expression other than the one given at childhood. Ability to switch from one belief system or mental arrangement to another, discarding the previously held arrangement.

Level Five: COMBINATION
Investigation and participation in several disciplines. The coming together of bits and pieces of varied mental arrangements. The beginning of reflection and the sweep of awareness.

Level Six: CREATIVE EXPRESSION
Direct contact between searcher and all that is witnessed. Expression beyond that which is memorized, recited or caused externally in any way. The disappearance of divisions between expressions.

Level Seven: PURE SEARCH
Expression is unimportant as consciousness races toward new realizations. There is now only discovery and expanding awareness.

Appendix II

STAGES OF INDIVIDUALIZED
HUMAN CONSCIOUSNESS

First Stage: Sensual awareness. Initial reality construction. Beginning of classification. Initial decisions.

Second Stage: Logging control factors into memory. Early decisions of separation. Personality begins.

Third Stage: Use of memory to establish division and proclaim importance. Systems fail. Disappointments begin.

Fourth Stage: Start of formal social training. Establish language, relative intelligence, physical abilities, etc.

Fifth Stage: Defiance of authority. Personality definition and social position investigated, perhaps decided.

Sixth Stage: Young adulthood. No conscious awareness of Mind. Ownership and competition. Proving image.

Seventh Stage: Joining in relationships, small groups and clubs. Competition and responsibility. Family attachments.

Eighth Stage: Organization participation. Social and volunteer activities. National participation.

Ninth Stage: Retirement. Family grown. Relaxation of ideas of ownership. Seeing through religious expression.

Tenth Stage: Completion of union with Mind. Loss of ideas of separation. Renewal of awareness.

Complete involvement in external differences								Awareness only of "self" and memories.	
Anxieties of condition, image and time								Overconcern with memory aging. Mistakes of real & ideal	
Concern with "self" image blaming others for errors & failures								Concern for appearances of self and family	
Importance of category groupings								Racial, social, ethnic & territorial superiority or inferiority	
Ownership								Personality concerns	
Importance of Gender								Sexual superiority or inferiority	
Knowledge of Good & Evil								Awareness of social program	
Communications								Language (ours, theirs)	
Sensual Awareness								Awareness of life and death	
Birth								End physical self	
1st stage	2nd stage	3rd stage	4th stage	5th stage	6th stage	7th stage	8th stage	9th stage	10th stage

Stages of Individuated Consciousness

Appendix III

Participtory Levels of Consciousness

Level 1: Psychosis. Complete separation from anything witnessed. Fixation and obsession. Total isolation.

Level 2: Neurosis. Body and body processes identification. Superiority or victimization. Concern for image and time.

Level 3: Religious Non-Seeking. Blame and guilt as social tool. Experience of accord. Family and group identification.

Level 4: Clergy. Authority. "Knower of right and wrong". Teacher of system rules and regulations. Director of rites.

Level 5: Religious Seeking. Doubt of religious authority. Investigation of alternative expressions.

Level 6: Philosophy. Questioning of basic concepts. Reflection of mental process. Contemplation of cause and effect.

Level 7. Spiritually Communicative. Knowing and expressing The Union of All Existence. Shared knowledge.

Level 8: Spiritually Non-Communicative. Borderline of life and death. Being and happening. Knower of Truth extending.

Level 9: Undifferentiated Spirit. Ground of Being. Truth. Union of All Existence. Nameless and limitless.

The amount of separation and level of participation are determined by the divisions made and held important by an aspect of consciousness. The greater the number and the more important the differences, the more psychotic the aspect.

What an aspect sees as powerful, giving itself more separation and definition, **Undifferentiated Spirit** sees as loss of power by entering into the conditional world. To the separated self, it is climbing the mountain of individuality where fame and fortune are assured. To Spirit it is descending into the *canyon of conceit*.

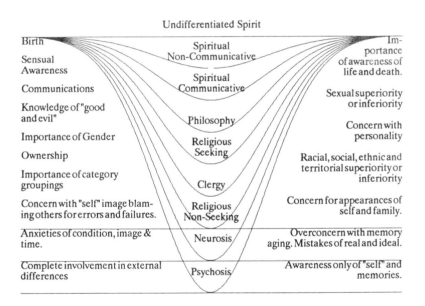

Degrees of Separation in Canyon of Conceit

Appendix IV

AWARENESS AND PURPOSE

Plateau Nine: Cosmic and Universe. Omniscience, Omnipresence and Omnipotence. Infinity and Eternity. Truth. Knowledge.

Plateau Eight: Living. Concern for all life forms. Environment. Biochemical balance. Harmony of living creatures.

Plateau Seven: Animal. Concern for mobility of life forms. Territory. Food and air supply. Instincts and reproduction.

Plateau Six: Human. Concern for survival of human abilities. Externalized evolution. Human creative involvement.

Plateau Five: Nation. Concern for territory and language. Competition between nations. Relative might. Economics.

Plateau Four: Organization. Concern for belief system, "religions", school, or club. Social process. System competition.

Plateau Three: Family or Small Group. Local and immediate concerns of daily interaction. Idioms, cant and slang.

Plateau Two: Individual. Concern for body, development and image. Comparative measurement to "others". Intellectuality.

Plateau One: Ego. Separation from witnessed material or events. Obsession and predisposition. Inability to change.

As aspect resolves conflicts at deeper levels within the canyon of conceit, divisions disappear and consciousness moves to the next higher plateau. Inclusion and increased awareness is the result of conflict resolution.

Possible Purposes	Plateau 9 - Undifferentiated Spirit	Increasing Awareness
Being and doing	Plateau 8 - Living	Man's relationship to world.
To influence. Evangelistic and Giving.	Plateau 7 - Animal	Concern for all animals.
Business, Politics. To lead.	Plateau 6 - Humanity	Comunity, Industrial, Recreational needs of humanity.
Patriot, "True Believer."	Plateau 5 - Nation	Denominational and Territorial awareness.
Family, "religion," and club.	Plateau 4 - Organization	Group or category awareness. Neighborhood.
Family or small group.	Plateau 3 - Family	Awareness of unity limited to family.
Home or a sport.	Plateau 2 - Individual	Constantly changing friends out of distrust.
Perpetuation.	Plateau 1 - Isolated Self	Total indulgence

Awareness and Purpose

Appendix V

SEASONS OF HUMAN DEVELOPMENT

First Season: Initial awareness. Primitive human. Externalization of evolution. Start of memory complexification.

Second Season: Beginning sight and sound communication. Lesser self permitted. Realization of life and non-life.

Third Season: Beginning verbal communications. Use of basic tools, skins and fibers. Separation from and use of animals.

Fourth Season: Separation from and suspicion of "other" human groups. Beginning of tribal conflict. Use of stone.

Fifth Season: Separation and identification of individuals. Competition for supremacy. Begin rule and regulation.

Sixth Season: Acceptance of rules. Group and tribal identities. Astro-science. Calendars. Written language. Religion.

Seventh Season: National identities. War for territories. Language and location separation. Fear of loss and death.

Eighth Season: Nations reach war limit. System failures. Corruption in education, government, religion. Pollution.

Ninth Season: Concern for other creatures. Continuity with animals. Environmental concerns. End of national hostilities.

Tenth Season: Union of Mind recognized. Consciousness tamed. Understanding achieved. Love realized. Humanity awakens.

1st season	2nd season	3rd season	4th season	5th season	6th season	7th season	8th season	9th season	10th season

Initial Awareness
Undifferentiated Spirit
Conscious cosmic awareness

Initial Consciousness. Late animal & Early human
Acceptance of humanity as complete

Conscious awareness of memory and mentality
Memory Tamed

Human and animal separation
Verbal communications
Reacceptance of humans as animals

Humans consider separation from nature
Concern for other creatures.

Humanity versus nature
Environmental awareness and concern for human longevity

Supremacy of humanity
Individual and group hostility.

SEASONS OF HUMAN DEVELOPMENT
Evolutionary Curve of Man's Spiritual and Conscious Progress

Appendix VI

RELIGIOUS TRACKS

The real purpose of religion is explanation and invitation. Where it deviates from its purpose it becomes separate and inadequate as a conveyor of truth message. Deviating farther and farther from the initiating expression, it rises into confusion and disorder requiring its followers to take on faith the message that it no longer heeds. Losing touch with the reason for its initial expression, the "religion" falls into the neurotic and psychotic levels of separation, often fighting other aspects of itself.

All religious expression starts from the same realization, the awareness that separation does not exist. No thing is really separate from any other thing. The prophet or person initiating the expression is at least partially aware of this truth. The expression, however, takes on the amount of separation, divisions and importances that are dictated by the mental arrangement of the expressing person and the interaction with the current social system. The realization and its expression cannot deviate far from the accepted standards of its time and still be relevant.

The religious tracks expressed here are not meant to be definitive or infallible. They are meant to be an aid to understanding.

Many "religious" expressions are not religious in nature but are, rather, organizational since their purpose is not to bring followers to an awareness of their total union with All Existence, but a realization of their separation and differences.

All religious expression eventually converges in the ninth and tenth seasons of human development.

Initial Awareness	Conscious cosmic awareness
Initial Consciousness. Late animal & Early human	Acceptance of humanity as complete
Conscious awareness of memory and mentality	Memory Tamed
Human and animal separation Verbal communications	Reacceptance of humans as animals
Humans consider separation from nature	Concern for other creatures.
Humanity versus nature	Environmental awareness and concern for human longevity
Supremacy of humanity	Individual and group hostility.

Religious Tracks on Human Destiny

Track One: Natural religion as practiced by indian tribes and primitive humans. Also Taoism and basic Pagan expressions.

Track Two: Hinduism, Buddhism, Shintoism and similar eastern expressions.

Track Three: Judaism.

Track Four: Christianity. Divisions could be shown for the followers of Jesus and other Christian expressions.

Track Five: Mideast religions. Islam, Mohammidanism and Bahai.

Track Six: Western religious expression and psycho-sciences.

163

Appendix VII

DISSEMINATION OF POWER

All aspects of Mind have the natural power of Mind at their disposal.

Giving Power: Those at the lowest levels in the Canyon of Conceit give their power to those at the next higher level and to all levels above. Most do so without realization of this process. Those at the bottom of the canyon must either muddle about in ignorance, blind to their role in cause of circumstance, using their power haphazardly or give it to those who are more aware.

Investing Power: Those who realize that trouble and illness are the result of ignorance find counterparts at higher levels of consciousness in which to invest their power. Being discriminating in their choice, they elect to invest power with those who, recognizing their union, return the power through enlightened guidance.

Receiving Power: Aspects of consciousness that receive power from those at lower levels within the Canyon of Conceit must be cautious of the use of this power, using it only in the investor's best interest. The receiving aspect may only use such power to aid the investing aspect in raising its level of awareness. To do otherwise is to destroy the accord and drop deeper into the canyon.

Appendix VIII

METHODS OF CHANGING DECISION

Deciding: Deciding is the process of choosing between two or more alternatives. Until an alternative is on the borderline of awareness, decision is impossible.

Making a Decision: Recognizing two or more alternatives, the aspect chooses one turning its back on the other. If the aspect is, for some reason, unable to do this, the aspect is unable to decide and cannot change awareness levels. This aspect must depend on an aspect at a higher level of awareness, closely following instructions, if it intends to change levels.

Decision Continuation: A decision that is not continued has not been made. Only a continued decision is effective in changing levels of awareness. Decisions are continued by keeping the decision before the eye of consciousness.

Methods of Decision Continuation: Prayer. Recitation. Affirmations. Engaging sensual perception in repetition. Employing another aspect as a reminding facility.

Changing from defective to effective creativity: Operation that is effective is caused by decision. Without the decision to operate from a place of agreement, the operation of an aspect is more likely to become defective.

When an aspect recognizes that it has been operating defectively and chooses to become more effectively creative, it is usually necessary to create a period of ineffective operation or non-action. This can be done through prayer, meditation, chanting or any of the numerous methods that take conscious attention away from its system of divisions and importances.

Following this, new, more appropriate divisions are made and declared important. Through this process, the aspect changes the world it witnesses and, therefore, its reaction to circumstance.